THE SWEDISH TABLE

THE SWED

ISH TABLE

Helene Henderson

COLOR PHOTOGRAPHY BY LISA RUTLEDGE
FOOD STYLING BY HELENE HENDERSON AND TREVOR ZIMMERMAN

UNIVERSITY OF MINNESOTA PRESS   MINNEAPOLIS · LONDON

Published by the University of Minnesota Press
111 Third Avenue South, Suite 290
Minneapolis, MN 55401-2520
http://www.upress.umn.edu

Library of Congress Cataloging-in-Publication Data

Henderson, Helene.
The Swedish table / Helene Henderson; color photography by Lisa Rutledge;
food styling by Helene Henderson and Trevor Zimmerman.
    p. cm.
ISBN 0-8166-4513-2 (hc/j : alk. paper)
1. Cookery, Swedish. 2. Sweden—Social life and customs. I. Title.
TX722.S8H47 2005
641.59485—dc22

                    2004028038

Printed in the United States of America on acid-free paper

The University of Minnesota is an equal-opportunity educator and employer.

12 11 10 09 08 07 06 05   10 9 8 7 6 5 4 3 2 1

In memory of my grandmother Jenny
and for my children, Celia, Casper, and Caden

Contents

FROM HEAVEN Hot and Chilled Soups

FROM THE EARTH Potatoes

FROM THE FOREST AND THE FARM Meat, Game, and Chicken

FROM THE SEA Fish and Shellfish

FROM THE GARDEN Vegetables and Salads

FROM THE DELI Sandwiches

FROM THE CHICKEN COOP Eggs, Waffles, and Pancakes

FROM THE OVEN # Desserts, Pastries, and Bread

FROM THE BAR # Beverages

FROM THE FOREST Wild Berry Preserves

Acknowledgments

I would first like to thank Todd Orjala, senior acquisitions editor at the University of Minnesota Press, for making this book a reality. I woke up one morning with the idea that I would write a cookbook about Sweden for my children, and I quickly hammered out a ten-page proposal that I dropped in the mail to the general editor of the University of Minnesota Press, which had already published several fine Scandinavian cookbooks. To my surprise Todd called, expressing enthusiastic interest. Without an agent or insider contacts, I had sent an unsolicited book proposal to a publishing house where someone had not only read it but believed in it. Truly America is the magic kingdom of dreams and possibilities. I also thank the rest of the team at the University of Minnesota Press, including Pieter Martin, Laura Westlund, Michele Hodgson, Adam Grafa, and Barbro Roehrdanz, for their expertise.

Thanks to Lisa Rutledge, who not only shot the beautiful color photographs in this book but also taught me how to prepare for each shoot by imagining everything from background colors to the shape of the plates to the presentation of the food. Thanks to Trevor Zimmerman for assisting with the food styling and to Elizabeth McDonald Reise for helping with Caden, my baby, so I could focus on the photographs. I thank my friend Myra Vides for taking the black-and-white publicity photographs

I thank my husband, John, for convincing me that everything is possible and that opportunities come to those who pursue them; he has always told me I can accomplish whatever I set my mind to. I thank my children; without their constant questions about Sweden I never would have come up with this idea in the first place. I thank my father-in-law, John Stockwell Samuels III, who read and corrected the first draft of the manuscript, and I thank my friend Donna Stia, who hired me to cater my first party and introduced me to Lisa Rutledge.

Finally, I thank my Swedish family—my mother, Harriet, and my aunt and uncle, Birgit and Harry Kempén—for teaching me about the magic of the forest, the lakes, and the farms of the Swedish heartland.

Introduction

Everything I know and love about food I learned at the end of the world in the tiny town of Luleå, Sweden, where I grew up. Every recipe in this book is based on my childhood food memories but pairs the finest ingredients, flavors, and scents from my past with produce, spices, and tastes of the present to create new dishes for (and to re-create old dishes from) the Swedish table.

As the sole African American amid a sea of blue-eyed blonds in Luleå, an industrial town in the very north of Sweden, I never physically fit in. My unruly Afro and tall, superskinny body did not help. But when I held summer's first potato just dug from the ground, or tasted the season's first ripe cloudberry, or smelled grilled salmon fresh off the boat, it did not matter what I looked like. I was Swedish, I was home, and I belonged.

My mother, a typical blond Swede, met my father, an African American jazz musician, while he was on tour in Scandinavia. They married and divorced in quick progression, then my father disappeared with his drum set, not to be seen or heard from for many years. I never saw another black person until I came to America.

I grew up with my mother's extended Swedish family. I lived with my grandmother because my mother worked late nights as a waitress. When I was older, I started working at the restaurant with her, chopping vegetables and learning the trade of cooking. On weekends I tended our little patch of organic potatoes and vegetables and used them to create my own recipes. Food became my friend and confidant, and cooking became my boyfriend, my sport of choice, my after-school job. Slowly, I became an expert in Swedish cooking.

From the time I was twelve until I was seventeen, I worked evenings and holidays at various restaurants in Luleå, where simple, home-style cooking was served. When the owner of the highly successful

Above: Before this photograph was taken, I spent hours flattening my stiff, unruly Afro into this semi-manageable style, but my hair still stood out distinctively from all the Swedish blonds around me.

Swedish hamburger chain Max Grillen (whose signature burgers were seasoned with Thousand Island dressing) opened a French bistro, Petite Maxine, in our town, I was hired as a waitress. The bistro served upscale French food at reduced prices, and ran at a loss from day one since our town of working-class families could not afford to support a high-end restaurant. The freestanding building, smack in the center of our main street, was designed as an oval garden conservatory with ornate, wall-to-wall white-framed windows. Inside, in the center of the room and surrounded by small round tables covered with white linens, was a sunken wine cellar. Every time wine was ordered, the cellar was opened with great fanfare and servers climbed down the stairs to retrieve the requested vintage. Fresh orange juice was made from a machine that cut whole oranges and squeezed the juice directly into a small glass. The restaurant was both a showcase and a circus, and it quickly became the most famous restaurant in the north of Sweden.

A talented and temperamental chef was brought up from Stockholm to head the kitchen. Not used to living in a town with nowhere to go and nothing to do, he became a complete drunk halfway through his first winter in Luleå. When I showed up for work in the mornings, I would find him passed out on the floor, surrounded by empty bottles. By then I was the sous chef, so I would begin the prep work myself, trying to copy what I had seen him do the day before. As the chef slept later and later each day, I began to master the basics of French cooking by necessity. The menu was bold, imaginative, and sophisticated, and soon I was serving dinners of potato gratin and roasted rack of venison with wild-mushroom sauce and snails roasted in herb butter. On Sundays I prepared gravlax omelets. The owner became my mentor and my friend.

In the 1970s, Luleå was a one-factory steel town and the industry was flourishing. A new, larger factory, Stålverk 80 (nicknamed "Playa Plannja"), was planned, and new homes and stores were built in anticipation. The bistro was packed every night. But when the steel industry crashed, the construction of Playa Plannja stopped, and most workers in the old factory were given their walking papers. Stores and restaurants, including the bistro, closed. An exodus began as the government offered incentives to the unemployed to move south, where jobs were available. The young especially had few prospects, so we left, one by one, after graduating from high school. Most of my friends went to Stockholm, while others left for a year in England to perfect their English and wait for the job market back home to improve. Encouraged by the bistro owner, I left for America in 1980 for what I thought would be one year—but I still am here today.

When I arrived in New York City with my one-way ticket and five hundred dollars in savings, I was seventeen, alone, and without a plan. But when you are young and naïve in a city like New York, things somehow work out. I never considered cooking or working in a restaurant; I was looking for more exciting things to do with my life, and soon I had a job in a clothing store. Once I even modeled for fashion designer Betsey Johnson. I still had a crazy head of hair, which fit right in with the wild-animal print designs of the show. I had grown up hiding behind others and constantly trying to blend in, and I felt uncomfortable in the spotlight. I recognized that modeling was not for me.

After a year in New York and two years modeling in Europe, I decided to try my luck in Los Angeles. Even though I had no graphic design experience, I worked as a title designer at Cannon Films, a job that Karyn Rachtman, my New York roommate, found for me. Karyn also set me up on a blind date with John Stockwell, a film director at Cannon Films. John soon became my husband and a fan of my Swedish cooking, which I prepared whenever we entertained friends at our small Hollywood home.

On the boat dock in Luleå with my mother in 1969. By the time I was twelve years old, I towered a full five inches over her petite frame.

One day my friend Donna Stia asked if I would help prepare the food for a party she was having. The dinner was a huge success, and soon other people were calling to ask me to prepare food for their special occasions. I never set out to return to cooking, but soon my calendar was booked with events. Before long I was heading my own company, Lavender Farms Catering.

As a caterer in Los Angeles, you cannot help but cook for famous people. At a dinner I catered for Steven Webber (a friend of Donna's), Madonna showed up and ate baby new potatoes I had made. Seated next to her was Kiefer Sutherland, and soon I was at his house torching rice pudding crème brûlées. I catered a dinner at the Malibu Stage Company, attended by none other than Barbra Streisand and James Brolin. Two weeks later I was making rosemary lamb chops at her fabulous Malibu estate, which was filled with celebrities—John Travolta, Kelly Preston, Kenny G, Woody Allen, and an unnamed VIP from Washington. As Secret Service agents swarmed the gated property, I wondered if President Clinton, who was in Los Angeles that weekend, was eating the Swedish lamb chops I had prepared for the party. As I drove home along Pacific Coast Highway, Ms. Streisand's home fading in the rearview mirror and the night air holding at a balmy 72 degrees (in February!), I could scarcely believe my luck. How could I have imagined back in Luleå when I was picking berries with my grandmother or catching fish with my uncle that I would end up serving foods of the Swedish forest and lakes to such glamorous people in America? I had traveled alone from the end of the world and found myself in the center of the universe. I knew that the American dream was no myth.

When I shop the farmers' markets near my home in Los Angeles, I look for produce that reminds me of my childhood. The vegetables and fruits here may look bigger and more varied, but they still have the power to transport me home with their earthy scents. Since leaving Sweden more than twenty years ago, I have been back many times. Luleå has slowly recovered from the economic troubles of its past, helped in part by the famed Ice Hotel north of town, which has attracted tourists to the area. New stores

My grandmother Jenny at the summerhouse, preparing the soil to plant Swedish Peanut potatoes, the star staple of Swedish cuisine.

have popped up, as have new restaurants. On Thursdays, however, you will still find savory yellow pea soup simmering on the stove in homes and restaurants, and fresh-baked bullar served at fika every day, everywhere, in anticipation of arriving guests.

Sweden is still the place of my heart, the place where food, family, and memories all come together. I hope this cookbook will bring a bit of my Sweden to you. Many of the recipes are not traditionally prepared, although instructions for Swedish-style preparation are often mentioned in the introductions to the recipes. Sometimes the original recipes are so delicious that any improvement is impossible, so I have included them as is, but most of the recipes take my cherished memories of Swedish food and incorporate them into modern California cooking, using widely available ingredients to create dishes that Swedes and Americans alike will enjoy. No matter where you are from, I hope the flavors and fragrances here will bring *you* home, too.

Swedish Holidays, Customs, and Celebrations

Sweden has two seasons: summer and winter, lightness and darkness. Likewise, the Swedes have two personalities that go along with those seasons: outgoing and vivacious, reserved and somber. In the summer, in celebration of the midnight sun, the otherwise quiet Swedes become fun-loving. They spend the season outside, rain or shine, and every meal is a festival of freshness and goodness from the earth and the sea. Winter brings bone-chilling cold, massive snowfall, and months of nearly twenty-four-hour darkness when the sun never rises over the horizon. Swedes spend the season inside, cocooned from the arctic air, and their mood turns gloomy.

Like all Swedes, I worshipped the sun and summer, which brought baby new potatoes—fragile, tender, creamy, the best in the world. I danced around the maypole and feasted on the fruits from the sea, forest, and garden. An entire afternoon would pass in an instant as I sat in the forest eating juicy and tart fresh berries, taking in the beauty of the land.

In the winter, I loved cross-country skiing through quiet, snow-covered forests and stopping for a picnic of smooth, salty gravlax sandwiches with a thermos of steaming rose hips soup. Returning home safely after a school field trip of ice-skating on the lake (having fearfully clutched my school-provided ice picks, which would save me if I plunged through the ice), I was comforted to find my grandmother waiting with semlor, light and fluffy buns filled with almond paste and whipped cream and nesting in a bowl of hot milk.

The Swedes survive the long winters with endearing customs and celebrations that help carry them out of the darkness and back to the delights of summer. Although not typically strongly religious, the Swedes follow such traditions (especially the festival of Santa Lucia) religiously. As the world becomes more unpredictable and lifestyles more global, they take comfort in customs that have been central to Swedish life for generations. They take great pride in their country and enjoy distinguishing themselves from their Scandinavian neighbors (particularly the Finns!). They pay their taxes with pride (in kronor, not euros). They observe the formal rules of fika (socializing) and skål (toasting). And they always arrive

Dressed as Santa Lucia in 1970, I bring fragrant saffron and raisin buns to my grandmother. Traditionally, the Santa Lucia crown should consist of real lit candles, but many safety-conscious Swedes now prefer battery-operated lights.

on time; in fact, punctuality is a national obsession. When invited as a guest to a Swedish home, make sure you arrive on time—it is quite an offense to arrive more than five minutes late. In addition, "I'll call you next week" or "Let's get together tomorrow" are taken literally in Sweden.

Although they are a deeply democratic people, the Swedes adore their constitutional monarchs, King Carl XVI and Queen Silvia (and their three children). Sweden may not be the largest or most powerful nation, but as the Swedes like to say, "Our home is our castle—and our country is our kingdom."

SANTA LUCIA Sweden's customs of the winter holidays start early in December with the beginning of Advent. Four tall candles nestle within an evergreen wreath in every home and church. On the first Sunday of Advent (usually the first Sunday in December) one Advent candle is lit, the second Sunday two are lit, and so on until all four candles are glowing, signaling that Christmas week has arrived.

The holiday season reaches full swing on December 13, traditionally believed to be the darkest night of the year. Certainly in the north of Sweden the sun stays below the horizon all day, creating a dreary time, when outdoor Christmas lights and candles provide the only bright spots in the snowbanked streets.

December 13 also marks the festival of Santa Lucia, the celebration of lights and longer days to come. It is believed that early missionaries brought the legend of Lucia to Sweden. Lucia was slain about A.D. 300 in Syracuse, Sicily, for her Christian beliefs. Her eyes were gouged, staining her virgin white dress with blood, represented today by a simple white gown and a red satin belt.

On the morning of December 13, the oldest daughter in each family portrays Lucia. In addition to the white gown and red belt, she wears a crown of flaming candles. Any younger daughters are her attendants, also wearing white gowns but tied with tinsel rope; they wear a headband instead of a crown and hold a single lit candle. Boys participate either as Santa's elves, wearing all red, or as Lucia boys (star boys), each wearing a white gown and a conical hat decorated with golden stars and carrying a wand topped with a large golden star. The children sing traditional songs as Santa Lucia dispels the darkness of winter by carrying a tray of homemade goodies to the parents before sunup: golden saffron buns (page 130), fragrant cinnamon rolls (page 136), buttery dream cookies (page 142), and spicy *pepparkakor* (ginger-snaps, page 143).

This scene is repeated at schools, hospitals, nursing homes, offices, and the royal palace, as well as on national television. Lucia competitions are held throughout Sweden, with the most beautiful girl selected to represent the school, the state, even the nation, like a Miss America. Many girls enter the prestigious (or at least emotional) pageant in hopes of being voted Lucia. Traditionally, the winner is a classic Scandinavian beauty with blue eyes and long, blond hair.

I especially treasured the festival of Santa Lucia and the enchantment of light and goodness she brings. One year, I, the skinny African American girl, was voted the Lucia of my class. For the first time, I wore the crown of lit candles over my bopping Afro while singing the words to the song that accompanies the procession, "Then in our darkened house, rises with candle lights, Santa Lucia, Santa Lucia"—completely out of tune. As much as I dreamed (and it *was* my fantasy), Diana Ross I was not.

CHRISTMAS Once Santa Lucia Day has passed, Christmas is right around the corner. Like all children, I loved that magical time. Houses and trees are decorated with evergreen garlands and twinkling white lights. Ice sculptures are made in the city center. In Sweden the holiday is celebrated on Christmas Eve. The festivities begin at three o'clock, when children and adults alike stop whatever they're doing to watch a two-hour televised show of Kalle Anka (Donald Duck). Year after year, the classic show stays the same; any changes to the program would cause mass protest. Christmas in Sweden does not begin until Kalle Anka dances, quacks, and pratfalls it in.

Then it is time for the real show: the unveiling of the dinner table. The Christmas ham—the *julskinka*—is the centerpiece, surrounded by aquavit (page 165) and dill-marinated gravlax (page 62), succulent tiny meatballs (page 49), boiled tender baby potatoes, an assortment of pickled herrings, lingonberry preserve (page 178), salads, and *wasa* crisp bread and an overflowing platter of sliced regional cheeses. For dessert there is rice pudding (page 150) with a lucky almond hidden inside, predicting marriage or newfound riches for whoever finds the prize. As always, a variety of freshly baked bullar (page 133) and cookies (pages 142–44) is served. After dinner there's a visit from the "tomten," a Christmas gnome who is believed to be a sprite that once lived under barns to protect the livestock. He comes to each house with small gifts and candy for the children.

At my aunt's home, where our family would gather for Christmas, the tomten would arrive on cross-country skis after dark. We would crowd around the window, waiting in anticipation, when suddenly his silhouette would appear, gliding gracefully on his skis and carrying a large sack on his back. First we watched him go inside the neighbors' house; after what seemed an eternity, we saw him come out, put his skis back on, and coast across the snow-covered lawn toward my aunt's home. Then loudly, while banging on the door, he would proclaim, "Ho, ho, ho!"

Terrified and thrilled, we threw open the door to receive his token gifts, then he disappeared into the darkness. I never knew who the tomten was. Was it my uncle, the neighbor, the mayor of our town—or

At home with my mother, Christmas 1969. While ham bakes in the oven, we eagerly await the arrival of the tomten, the Swedish Christmas gnome.

was this really a sprite who protected us? What I know for certain is that he is Sweden's magical, mythical, noncommercial Santa figure.

In Sweden the majority of Christmas gifts are given and received by family and friends, and opened before the arrival of the tomten. After dessert is served, the enchanting evening comes to an end.

Christmas Day is a low-key affair, a time for family and friends to gather around a smörgåsbord of foods, many the same as those served the night before but presented differently, and often including lutfisk—dried, soaked, and boiled lingcod covered with a silky white sauce—and *dopp i grytan*—freshly baked limpa (page 153), a soft rye bread studded with golden and black raisins, which is dipped in the savory, salty broth used to boil the Christmas ham. This act commemorates the meager times in old Sweden when no part of a meal could go to waste, and celebrates the end of the old year and the hope of the new year to bring light, warmth, hope, and prosperity.

SHROVE TUESDAY Religion has fallen to the wayside for most Swedes, who visit church mainly for christenings, confirmations, weddings, and funerals. Many Swedes still maintain the tradition of eating heartily on Shrove Tuesday, just before the Lenten season of fasting begins—except that no one bothers to fast after indulging in the feast!

Succulent roasted pork (page 46) with baked brown beans with syrup and vinegar (page 93) and my all-time, must-eat, ultimate treat, semlor (page 131)—also known as Fat Tuesday buns—are eaten at this time, ideally in a bowl of warm milk. Semlor originally may have been eaten to prepare for the beginning of fasting for Lent, but for most Swedes its sweet, intoxicating almond flavor assures them that spring and sunshine are on the way.

EASTER Bunnies are conspicuously absent in the Swedish celebration of Easter, a holiday more reminiscent of Halloween. Swedish folklore holds that on Maundy Thursday witches would steal all household brooms to fly off to Blåkulla (Blue Mountain), somewhere out in the Baltic Sea, where they would pay their respects to the devil for a feast he hosted. Based on this legend, children dress up like witches, ride on brooms through the neighborhood, and shout, "Glad Påsk!" ("Happy Easter!") in return for coins and treats. I would imagine I was Diana Ross, not a witch, and I would fly past Blue Mountain on my broomstick, head west over the Atlantic, and arrive in the land of the free and the home of the brave, where my Afro and I would blend right in.

Halibut (page 71) is the customary entrée for Good Friday, and lamb (page 44) is frequently served on Easter Sunday. On Maundy Thursday my grandmother would make the traditional emerald green seven-herb nettle soup (page 11) and garnish it with chopped hard-boiled eggs. Together, she (an ancestor of the Vikings) and I (in my Miss Ross getup) would ward off any and all evil spirits in our tiny two-room walk-up apartment. Later, we would walk to the neighborhood bonfire, where people had gathered at dusk while children set off firecrackers, and we would watch the dark night and warm our spirits. The bonfires are believed to offer protection from the devil and the witches.

The beginning of summer had arrived.

MIDSUMMER'S DAY The midsummer celebration takes place on the weekend nearest to June 24, believed to be the longest day of the year. In northern Sweden this is the time of the midnight sun, when the sun never sets and people stay out all night. Homes and churches are decorated with wildflower garlands and flowering tree branches, and an elaborately decorated maypole takes center stage. All night long young and old, dressed in regional costumes, dance around the pole. Young people pick flowers and put them under their pillows in hopes of dreaming of their future bride or groom.

Even though I put wildflowers under my pillow each midsummer night, I never had a special dream of my future mate. I dreamed only of baby new potatoes fresh from the garden, gleaming fish right out of the wild rivers, and ripe, bright, juicy berries from the forest—a midsummer night's dream for a food lover.

Summer ends with the crayfish festival, which begins August 14 and lasts three weeks. The tiny crustaceans are caught in freshwater, boiled with dill, eaten with potatoes, buttered toast, and cheese, and washed down with schnapps and beer. All too soon, it is the end of summer.

FIKA The most important custom in Sweden is the art of fika. The day begins and ends with fika, and it also happens many times between, while you talk about the weather, the all-time favorite topic of conversation for most Swedes (in the north, at least).

Fika means taking coffee and sweets, but it is more than that. It is a social event, it is a way of life, it establishes who your true friends are and where you stand with them. A simple fika could be a quick cup of coffee and a small cookie or pastry. An elaborate fika involves numerous varieties of cookies, pastries, tarts, and sweets. The more important the occasion or the guest, the fancier the fika. Swedish bullar (page 133) is the most significant component of fika. Bullar are sweet, chewy, and moist yeast-dough buns flavored with butter, cinnamon, cardamom, and pearl sugar.

My mother and my aunt skinny dipping under the midnight sun at the summer-house. Chilled aquavit, beer, and hot Gruyère and béchamel sandwiches await them after the swim.

I remember climbing the stairs in my aunt's apartment building, the smell of freshly baked bullar filling the hallway, the scent of heaven and earth beckoning me inside. And because my aunt would always make bullar for my weekly visit, I felt special—I was somebody important to her. My children, who met my aunt only twice before she passed away, still remember how her kitchen smelled of oven-fresh bullar. She was the champion of fika.

Although my mother has been coming to visit me in America for more than ten years, she is still not convinced I have any real friends here. Why? Because when we visit them, they do not offer us an elaborate fika. We are lucky (per American custom) to get a drink or a cup of coffee and maybe bagels. (Bagels? Where are the home-baked goodies?) And I must not like my friends much in return since I don't prepare fika for *them*. And what does it mean when I haven't prepared fika for my own mother?

My mother takes fika three to six times per day. Depending on what she eats for breakfast, it could be considered fika (coffee and a cinnamon roll qualifies, cereal does not). Shortly after arriving at work, employees declare in unison that it is time for fika and off to the office lunchroom they go. One hour later it is lunchtime, when dessert might include a quick fika. A few hours after lunch, it is most definitely fika time again. (I am not sure how Sweden operates as efficiently as it does with the constant fika breaks—and the eight-week paid vacations—its workforce enjoys. There must be magic ingredients in fika that somehow increase productivity in fewer hours.) Then my mother eats dinner early, around five o'clock (very common in Sweden, in part, I am sure, to squeeze in one more fika afterward). Shortly after dinner there is the final fika before bed. And so the days repeat.

I have to admit that, more than two decades after leaving Sweden, I have a three o'clock craving for fika that cannot be satisfied with a bagel or a Snickers bar. It is not just the sugar I crave, it is the ritual of fika, the intoxicating scent of bullar, the knowledge that you are a special guest and someone has made fika for you.

To make guests feel special in your home, make the Swedish bullar recipe on page 133 just before they arrive. Except for the breads, all recipes in the dessert section (pages 129–54) are suitable for fika.

My grandmother picks glorious wild berries that we will eat with whipped cream and freshly baked shortcakes.

You need a minimum of three items to ensure your Swedish guests will not be insulted. To impress, serve a variety of seven freshly baked items—and be ready to talk about the weather.

SMÖRGÅSBORD The smörgåsbord knows no season, no culinary boundaries, but it comes with plenty of customs. This is no leftovers meal—everything is made fresh. And unlike an American all-you-can-eat buffet, where diners overload their plates on the first run and mix all the courses at once, the Swedish smörgåsbord is eaten in a specific order, each trip to the buffet requiring a clean, small plate.

The smörgåsbord begins with multiple varieties of pickled herring: with mustard sauce, pickled red onions, and cracked black pepper, with curry and sour cream sauce, with sherry and tomatoes, and many more sumptuous variations. Boiled baby new potatoes seasoned with dill are served with the herring. A vast array of assorted cheeses—Ambrosia, Brie, Emmentaler, Gruyère, Svecia, and perhaps Stilton—is served with *wasa* crisp bread.

The next trip to the buffet is for gravlax (page 61) or fresh salmon (pages 64–67), again served with baby new potatoes. The third trip is for cold meats, such as ham and salami, and for pâté, salads, and egg dishes.

Just when you think the meal is over, you realize it has only begun. A fresh stack of clean plates indicates it is now time for the hot foods: meatballs (page 49), Jansson's Temptation (page 29), roasted lamb (page 44), cabbage rolls (page 70), and more. Lingonberries and more potatoes accompany the hot foods.

When the end of the meal finally arrives, the stars of Swedish cuisine—the desserts and sweets—come out: perhaps apple cake (page 149) with vanilla sauce or Swedish cheesecake (page 145) with cloudberries, assorted cookies, and freshly baked bullar. The feasting ends with strongly brewed coffee.

Throughout the smörgåsbord you drink aquavit (page 165) or beer while proclaiming "Skål!" ("Bottoms up!") after each trip to the buffet table.

*My aunt teaches my daughter Celia
the secrets and magic of bullar.*

THE ART OF SKÅL No matter where you are in Sweden, no matter what you eat, you will need to skål. If you are a guest at a Swedish dinner party and you are seated at the table, do not begin to drink until the host raises his glass high and proclaims, "Skål!" This indicates that the party has officially begun. For the rest of the evening, anyone and everyone at the table can (and will) proclaim skål every other minute. The most important part of the toast is that you connect with the host and fellow guests by making direct eye contact, both before and after raising your glass and taking a sip. Swedes, who ordinarily avoid eye contact, become more gregarious and vivacious with each drink.

To Swedish cooking—to the potato and to bullar, to the delicious treasures from the land and the sea—skål!

THE SWEDISH TABLE

Hot and Chilled Soups

Hot savory soups on a cold winter's night and cold sweet soups on a warm summer's day are a taste of heaven. The soups of my childhood were not only rich and filling, but soothing. They made the traumas and tribulations of my youth vanish.

As a child I always felt self-conscious because I was too skinny, too tall, too awkward. Strangers would stop my blond, blue-eyed mother in the street and say, "Bless you, bless you," as they shook her hand because they believed she had adopted me from Biafra, where a long drought had led to massive starvation among its people. Images of famished children with bulging bellies and hollow eyes filled the news.

She tried to beef me up, of course, raising me on potatoes, butter, and cream, but I stayed skinny. My mother would say, "Don't worry. When you go through puberty, you'll gain weight." Puberty came and went, I sprouted six inches, and still I was skinny. Pregnancy, I was guaranteed, would most definitely change my figure. Three kids later, I remain skinny.

But my self-consciousness disappeared with that first luscious spoonful of soup. When my grandmother expertly stirred thick cream into my bowl and pushed the fragrant soup toward me, the world consisted only of me, my grandmother, and that heaven-sent meal.

Most of the savory soup recipes in this book include potatoes, the Swedish staple, the all-time comfort food. Potato-based soups combined with seasoned broth and baby spring vegetables are the perfect meal any time of day. The sweet soups, made with berries and fruits from the forest or the garden, are refreshing and tangy. Fruit soups may be served hot or cold. Chilled fruit soup is usually eaten at lunch or as a snack. It also makes a refreshing ice-blended drink.

The cream has been greatly reduced or omitted in most of these recipes, and while they still taste sublimely delicious, they are healthy. But for a trip back in time, generously pour a serving of ice-cold heavy cream or milk into the sweet soups (rose hips, blueberry, rhubarb) or add cream to the savory soups (except the vegetable and red beet soups).

Chilled Rose Hips Soup with Whipped Cream

NYPONSOPPA SERVES 4–6

Rose hips are the fruit of roses, and rose hips soup is a great delicacy among the Swedes. Served hot out of a thermos, it is often packed for cross-country skiing outings. Served cold, it is garnished with whipped cream and almonds. Rose hips soup is the original sports drink, full of vitamin C, and is delicious served as an ice-blended beverage. Rose hips are available at most well-stocked health food stores.

1 cup dried organic rose hips
6 cups cold water
⅓ cup sugar
¼ cup fresh orange juice (optional)
1 tablespoon raspberry syrup (optional)
1 cup heavy cream, whipped until soft peaks form (optional)
1 cup slivered almonds (optional)

Raspberry Syrup (optional):
½ cup raspberries or strawberries
4 tablespoons sugar
1 tablespoon water

In a medium saucepan, combine rose hips and water. Simmer for 1 hour. Add ⅓ cup sugar and let mixture cool in the pan for 30 minutes.

Using an immersion blender (or a conventional blender), process the mixture until smooth. Strain mixture through a medium mesh strainer into a pitcher or storage container; discard the solids. For a thinner consistency, add 1 cup water. For a sweeter taste, add orange juice or raspberry syrup.

To make raspberry syrup, cook raspberries, sugar, and water for 5 minutes. Blend until smooth.

Cover and refrigerate the soup overnight. Ladle soup into bowl, garnish with whipped cream and almonds (optional), or pour a generous ladle of cold heavy cream or milk to serve with the soup.

Variation SERVES 2

For ice-blended drink: In a blender, combine 2 cups ice with 2 cups cold rose hips soup and blend until ice is incorporated. Pour into glasses and garnish with a heaping dollop of whipped cream and a sprinkling of almonds (optional).

Chilled Blueberry Soup
with Citrus-Infused Crème Fraîche

BLÅBÄRSSOPPA SERVES 4–6

Blueberry soup is an instant pick-me-up, healthier than a coffee drink and tastier than a smoothie. Traditionally, it is eaten with a generous serving of cold heavy cream. My grandmother would pour a small ladle of the thick, tangy soup into my bowl, then cover it with a big ladle of chilled heavy cream. I would dreamily swirl my spoon, mixing the blue soup into the white cream to create a simple yet luxurious treat. This recipe may be garnished with crème fraîche, a healthier alternative to cream.

3 cups blueberries
4 cups cold water
¾ cup sugar
1 vanilla bean, split in half lengthwise
1 large sprig of fresh mint

Garnish (optional):
½ cup crème fraîche or sour cream
1 tablespoon sugar
juice of ½ lemon (1 ½ tablespoons)
juice of ½ lime (1 tablespoon)
or
½ cup heavy cream, whipped until soft peaks form
fresh mint

In a medium saucepan, combine blueberries, water, and ¾ cup sugar. Cook over medium heat until soup begins to thicken, about 8–10 minutes. Turn off the heat, add the vanilla bean and mint, and let steep for 30 minutes. Remove vanilla bean and scrape the seeds into the blueberry mixture; discard the bean pod and mint. Using an immersion blender (or a conventional blender), process the mixture until smooth. Strain mixture through a fine mesh strainer into a pitcher or storage container; discard the solids. Cover and refrigerate soup.

While the soup is cooking, mix crème fraîche with 1 tablespoon sugar and lemon and lime juice. Garnish soup with crème fraîche, cold heavy cream, or milk if desired.

Variations SERVES 2

For hot soup: Simmer over medium heat. Serve in a coffee mug.

For ice-blended drink: In a blender, combine 2 cups ice with 2 cups cold blueberry soup and blend until ice is incorporated. Pour into glasses and garnish with a heaping dollop of whipped cream and mint (optional).

Vanilla Rhubarb Soup

RABARBERSOPPA SERVES 4–6

My aunt had a small rhubarb patch in her garden. The long and shiny cherry-red stalks grew abundantly in the cool Swedish climate. Immersed in the shade of the two-foot-high plant, I sat and chewed on the raw, tart fruit. After harvesting the rhubarb, we would make this delicious vanilla-flavored soup, as well as tangy desserts (page 152) and drinks (page 163).

4 ½ cups rhubarb (about 1 pound), coarse ends trimmed and discarded
2 cups water
¾ cup sugar
½ vanilla bean
1 tablespoon cornstarch, dissolved in 1 tablespoon water
3 tablespoons raspberry syrup (optional; page 4)

Cut rhubarb stalks into 1-inch pieces. In a medium saucepan, combine rhubarb, water, and sugar. Simmer over low heat until rhubarb starts to break apart, about 10–15 minutes. Add vanilla bean and let steep for 30 minutes. Remove vanilla bean and scrape the seeds into the rhubarb mixture; discard the bean pod. Whisk in dissolved cornstarch. While stirring, cook over low heat until soup begins to thicken, about 2–3 minutes. For a sweeter taste, add raspberry syrup. Serve immediately with cold heavy cream or milk.

Variation

For cold soup: Transfer cooked soup to pitcher or storage container. Cover and refrigerate overnight. Serve with cold heavy cream or milk.

Yellow Pea Soup with Bacon, Cherry Tomatoes, and Parsley

ÄRTSOPPA SERVES 6–8

Tired of *ER* and takeout Chinese on Thursday night? Join all Swedes—including the royal family—by making Thursday night yellow pea soup night. This smooth, savory soup is considered Sweden's national dish. Rumored to be King Gustaf's favorite meal, yellow pea soup was used to assassinate Swedish king Erik XIV, who, on a Thursday back in the late 1500s, was served a bowlful laced with arsenic.

Traditionally prepared with smoked pork shank, this lighter version of yellow pea soup is cooked with chicken stock and garnished with a sprinkling of bacon and chopped cherry tomatoes. But if you like the flavor of pork, that variation on the theme appears on the next page. Yellow pea soup is traditionally made with Swedish yellow peas (which first must be soaked overnight) and eaten with Swedish pancakes as dessert (page 118).

1 tablespoon olive oil
1 medium onion, peeled and chopped
1 carrot, peeled and chopped
1 celery stalk, chopped
2 cups dried yellow split peas (1 pound), soaked overnight
4 cups chicken broth (1 quart)
2 cups water
1 dried bay leaf
½ pint cherry tomatoes, chopped fine
1 clove garlic, peeled and minced
2 tablespoons olive oil
¼ cup fresh flat-leaf parsley, chopped
6 slices bacon, preferably apple-wood smoked, cooked crisp and crumbled
salt and pepper to taste

In a medium pot, combine olive oil, onion, carrot, and celery. Cook over medium heat, stirring occasionally, until vegetables begin to soften, about 5–8 minutes. Add peas, broth, water, and bay leaf. Bring to a boil, reduce to simmer, and cook according to package directions or until peas are tender, about 1 hour. Add more water if needed. Season with salt and pepper. Using an immersion blender (or a conventional blender) process soup until smooth. The soup will be very thick: thin soup by adding water or broth if desired.

While peas are cooking, mix tomatoes with olive oil, garlic, parsley, and salt and pepper to taste in a small bowl. Let marinate at room temperature for 1 hour. Ladle soup into bowls, add a generous tablespoon of marinated tomatoes in the center, and sprinkle with cooked bacon.

Variation

To serve with pork shank: Omit chicken broth, increase water to 6 cups, and add 1 ½ pounds pork shank. After cooking, remove and discard shank bone, cut or shred the pork, and return meat to the soup. Omit bacon garnish.

Vegetable Soup with Prosciutto-Filled "Gnocchi"

GRÖNSAKSSOPPA MED KROPPKAKOR SERVES 4–6

The most popular traditional vegetable soup in Sweden is *Kung Karl:s Kålsoppa* (King Karl's cabbage soup), which is made with white cabbage and seasoned with bay leaf. Although this particular version is made with carrot, celery, tomato, and spinach, you can add white cabbage or any of your favorite vegetables to the broth along with delicious *kroppkakor*—chewy, salty potato dumplings traditionally served with melted butter and lingonberries. For a lighter, more contemporary effect, this recipe places the dumpling mixture in a wonton wrapper, which is steamed and then served in the fragrant vegetable broth. Together, they make a deeply satisfying meal.

Dumplings:
1 cup russet baking potatoes (½ pound), peeled and cut into large chunks
1 tablespoon butter
1 tablespoon heavy cream
salt and coarsely ground black pepper to taste
½ pound bacon (8 slices), prosciutto, pancetta, or other ham
1 small onion, peeled and chopped fine
10 wonton wrappers or gyoza/shao mai *wrappers*
large lettuce leaves, such as romaine, to line steamer

Vegetable Soup:
2 tablespoons olive oil
1 large carrot, peeled and sliced thin
1 stalk celery, sliced thin
1 leek (white part only), chopped fine
4 cups chicken or vegetable broth (1 quart)
2 tomatoes, peeled, seeded, and diced
2 cups baby spinach (½ pound), washed
2 sprigs fresh flat-leaf parsley
juice of ½ lemon (1 ½ tablespoons)
salt and pepper to taste
dumplings

To make dumplings: In a medium pot, cook potatoes in salted water until soft, about 10 minutes. Drain and press potatoes through a ricer. Stir in butter and cream. Season with salt and pepper to taste. In a small sauté pan, cook bacon and onion over medium heat until bacon is crisp and onion is soft, about 3–4 minutes. Season with additional pepper to taste.

Spread wonton wrappers on a flat surface. Put 1 small tablespoon of the potato mixture in the center of each wrapper and top with 1 teaspoon of onion-bacon mixture. Moisten wrapper edges with water, fold to create a small purse, and pinch top edges to tighten seal. (For a more decorative dumpling, tie the top with a steamed chive.) Set a steamer basket in a small, shallow pan filled with an inch of water. Line the bottom of the basket with lettuce and place dumplings on top. Cover and simmer on low heat until dumplings are heated through, about 5 minutes. Serve drizzled with sweet melted butter and lingonberries (page 178) or with vegetable soup.

To make soup: In a large pot combine olive oil, carrot, celery, and leek. Cook over medium heat, stirring occasionally, until vegetables begin to soften, about 5–8 minutes. Season vegetables with salt and pepper to taste. Add broth and bring to a gentle boil over medium heat for 5 minutes. Stir in tomatoes, spinach, and parsley and let simmer 5 minutes more. Season with additional salt and pepper if needed. Add lemon juice. Place dumplings in a bowl and pour a ladle of soup over them.

Variations

For vegetarian dumplings: For bacon, substitute mixed mushrooms, minced and cooked.

For traditional dumplings: Mix 1 pound cooked and riced baking potato with 1 egg and 1 cup flour. Season with salt and pepper. Form potato mixture into a log and chill. Cut into a dozen quarter-inch sections, and stuff a small amount of cooked bacon and onion in the center and enclose. Cook dumplings in salted water about 5 minutes.

Note: Dumplings can be made, steamed, and chilled the day before serving. Reheat by steaming for a few minutes.

Nettle, Sorrel, and Baby Spinach Soup with Garlic Croutons

NÄSSELSOPPA **SERVES 4–6**

According to Swedish folklore, nettle soup—when served on Maundy Thursday (page xxiii)—is believed to ward off evil spirits, especially if you use seven different greens and herbs in the preparation. No matter what you believe about witches and broomsticks, the soup is guaranteed to ward off one unhealthy dinner and reward you with a delicious, simple meal.

This emerald-colored soup can be made with any assortment of greens, including butter lettuce, kale, arugula, parsley, and cilantro. Using freshly picked spring nettles, however, makes this soup a true delicacy. But take care: nettles are covered in tiny fibers that irritate the skin on contact, and they must be cooked to destroy their stinging effect. To collect nettles in the wild, wear gloves and use scissors to harvest only young shoots and leaf tops.

Nettle soup is typically garnished with hard-boiled eggs, although this recipe calls for homemade garlic croutons.

Soup:
1 tablespoon olive oil
1 medium onion, peeled and chopped
1 pound russet potatoes (1 large), peeled and chopped
2 cups chicken or vegetable broth
4 cups fresh nettle, sorrel, and baby spinach (1 pound total), rinsed,
*   stems removed, and torn into bite-size pieces*
juice of ½ lemon (1 ½ tablespoons)
salt and pepper to taste
garlic croutons, purchased or homemade (optional)

Garlic Croutons:
3 tablespoons butter
1 tablespoon olive oil
1 ½ cups day-old sourdough bread (2 thick slices), crusts removed and cut into cubes
1 garlic clove, peeled and minced fine
2 tablespoons fresh flat-leaf parsley, chopped fine
salt and pepper

To make soup: In a large pot, combine olive oil, onion, and potatoes. Cook over low to medium heat, stirring often, until onion is translucent and potatoes begin to soften but before they turn brown, about 6–8 minutes. Season with salt and pepper to taste. Add broth and bring to a boil, then simmer until potatoes are fully cooked, about 5–8 minutes more. Stir in nettle/herb mixture and cook for 5 minutes. Remove from heat, transfer soup into a blender, and process until smooth. Return soup to stockpot, add lemon juice, and add salt and pepper if needed. Ladle into bowls and garnish with croutons if desired.

To make croutons: In a small skillet, combine butter and olive oil and cook over medium heat until butter is melted. Add bread cubes and toss well. While stirring, cook until bread has absorbed the butter and starts to brown, about 3–5 minutes. Add garlic and parsley and stir until well combined. Drain croutons on paper towels and season lightly with salt and pepper.

Asparagus and Yukon Gold Potato Soup with Roasted Tomatoes

SPARRISSOPPA **SERVES 4**

This colorful soup is simple yet delicious, a celebration of spring. Made with fresh spring potatoes, chicken broth, and the tender, purple-tinged tips of asparagus, it is seasoned with a refreshing hint of lemon.

2 tablespoons olive oil
1 pound Yukon gold or russet potatoes (1 large), peeled and chopped
1 small onion, peeled and chopped
1 pound asparagus (about 16–20 spears), rough ends discarded and tops diced into medium chunks
2 cups chicken or vegetable broth
juice of 1 lemon (3 tablespoons)
salt and pepper

Garnish (optional):
4 Roma tomatoes, cored and cut in half
1 teaspoon canned chipotle pepper in adobo sauce or hot pepper sauce
1 teaspoon Worcestershire sauce
1 teaspoon balsamic vinegar
dash of sugar

In a large pot combine olive oil, potatoes, and onion. Cook over low to medium heat, stirring often, until onion is translucent and potatoes begin to soften but before they turn brown, about 6–8 minutes. Add asparagus and cook 2–3 minutes more. Season lightly with salt and pepper. Add broth and simmer until potatoes and asparagus are just done, about 3 minutes. Using an immersion blender (or a conventional blender), process soup for a few seconds until well blended but still chunky. Add lemon juice and, if needed, salt and pepper.

To make garnish: While soup is cooking, broil tomatoes, cut side down, until lightly seared and skins begin to curl. (Or, with a small amount of oil in a small skillet, cook tomatoes cut side up until lightly seared and skins begin to curl.) Peel and discard tomato skins and transfer tomatoes to a food processor. Add chipotle pepper, Worcestershire sauce, vinegar, and sugar. Process until mixture is smooth. Season with salt and pepper to taste.

Ladle asparagus soup into bowl and garnish with a generous tablespoon of tomato mixture.

Potato and Leek Soup with Fried Parsley

POTATIS OCH PURJOLÖKSSOPPA SERVES 4–6

Potato and leek soup is traditionally thought of as a French concoction, which it very well may be. But the potato is the key player, the lead violin, in the orchestra of Swedish cuisine, and any dish that prominently features potatoes is one to which the Swedes may claim proprietorship. Butter, potatoes, and cream are the makings of a good life—and the makings of a great soup.

My grandmother used to add a cup of heavy cream to this recipe, making it super rich, but I have reduced the amount to just a tablespoon, enough to add silkiness while keeping it light.

2 tablespoons butter
1 tablespoon olive oil
2 leeks (2 cups), white part only, chopped fine
2 pounds russet potatoes (2 large), peeled and chopped
6 cups chicken or vegetable broth
1 tablespoon fresh lemon juice
1 tablespoon heavy cream (optional)

Garnish (optional):
1 cup vegetable oil
¾ cup fresh flat-leaf parsley, chopped

In a large pot, melt butter with olive oil over medium heat. Add leeks and cook until translucent, about 5–8 minutes. Add potatoes and toss with the leeks. Salt and pepper to taste. Add broth and simmer until potatoes are soft, about 30–40 minutes. With an immersion blender (or a conventional blender), process soup until smooth. Stir in lemon juice and, if desired, cream. Add salt and pepper to taste.

To make garnish: While the soup is cooking, heat oil in a small skillet so that it is hot but not smoking. Slowly add parsley, first making sure it is completely dry before adding so the oil does not spatter. Fry the parsley, turning once, until bubbles subside. Remove parsley from the oil, drain on paper towels, and season with salt and pepper. Reserve oil for other use or discard. Ladle soup into bowls and garnish with fried parsley.

Red Beet Soup with Carrots and Balsamic Vinegar

RÖDBETSSOPPA **SERVES 4–6**

A savory soup without potatoes? For a Swede, that is difficult to imagine, but this refreshing variation on borscht pulls it off by taking advantage of tangy beets and carrots, sister vegetables from the soil. This gorgeous, ruby-red soup may be eaten hot or cold, with sour cream as a garnish if you wish.

4 tablespoons olive oil, divided
4 medium beets (1 ½ pounds, or 2 ½ cups)
2 tablespoons butter
2 medium onions, peeled and chopped
3 large carrots, peeled and chopped
2 cups chicken or vegetable broth
½ cup fresh orange juice
salt and pepper to taste
½ bunch fresh flat-leaf parsley, chopped (optional)

Preheat oven to 275 degrees Fahrenheit. In a small baking dish, combine 2 tablespoons oil and beets. Toss, cover with aluminum foil, and bake until soft when pierced, about 1 hour (or cover beets with foil and roast on an outdoor grill). Let cool, then peel the beets and dice into medium-size pieces.

While the beets are baking, combine butter with remaining 2 tablespoons olive oil in a pot. Cook over medium heat until butter is melted. Add onions and cook until translucent, about 5 minutes. Add carrots and cook for 2 minutes more. Season with salt and pepper to taste.

Add broth and simmer for about 30 minutes. Add cooked beets. Using an immersion blender (or a conventional blender), process soup until smooth. Add orange juice and season with additional salt and pepper to taste. Ladle soup into bowls and garnish with parsley.

Lentil Soup with Roasted Garlic and Baby New Potatoes

LINSSOPPA SERVES 4–6

My love for potatoes always makes me look for ways to combine them with other starches: pasta with potatoes, couscous with potatoes, beans with potatoes. Any grain or starch can and will be improved with the addition of potatoes. This recipe adds potatoes to lentils for a simple yet hearty country soup.

4 slices bacon, preferably apple-wood smoked, cut into thin, crosswise strips
1 large carrot (¾ cup), peeled and diced fine
1 celery stalk (½ cup), diced fine
1 small onion, peeled and diced fine
2 cups brown lentils
4 cups chicken or vegetable broth
4 cups water
½ cup olive oil, or enough to cover garlic cloves
6 cloves garlic, peeled
salt and pepper to taste
¾ pound baby new potatoes (about 10), boiled and quartered
½ bunch fresh flat-leaf parsley, chopped

Preheat oven to 250 degrees Fahrenheit. In a large pot, cook bacon over medium heat until browned and crispy; drain on paper towels. Cook carrots, celery, and onion in bacon fat until they begin to soften, about 4–5 minutes. Add lentils, broth, and water. Bring to a boil and simmer according to package directions or until lentils are just done, about 20 minutes.

In a small baking dish, combine oil and garlic. Cover dish with aluminum foil and bake until garlic is soft and lightly browned, about 30 minutes. Drain garlic; discard oil or save for other use. Stir garlic into soup.

Using an immersion blender (or a conventional blender), process soup for a few seconds, blending some of the lentils and vegetables but leaving most of the soup unblended and chunky. Return soup to pot and salt and pepper to taste. Stir in potatoes. Garnish with bacon and parsley.

Grilled Fish Soup with Saffron and Bacon

FISKSOPPA MED BACON SERVES 4–6

This saffron-infused soup makes great use of leftover grilled fish. The saffron gives the fragrant broth its vibrant color.

1 ½ to 2 pounds grilled or cooked assorted seafood: salmon (pages 64–67), swordfish, shrimp
6 slices bacon, preferably apple-wood smoked, cut into medium slices
1 small onion, peeled and chopped
1 celery rib, cut into ½-inch pieces
1 red bell pepper, cored, seeded, and chopped fine
salt and pepper to taste
1 cup fresh or frozen corn
1 cup dry white wine
8 ounces bottled clam juice
2 cups water
1 cup half-and-half
1 pinch saffron
juice of ½ lemon (1 ½ tablespoons)
dash of Tabasco
1 pound baby new potatoes (about 12, or 2 cups), cooked and cut in half
¼ cup fresh flat-leaf parsley, chopped

Cut grilled fish into bite-sized cubes. In a medium pot cook the bacon until crisp, about 5 minutes; drain on paper towels and set aside. Leave 1 tablespoon of fat in the pan; discard the rest. Cook onion, celery, and red pepper in the bacon fat until they begin to soften, about 2–3 minutes. Season with salt and pepper. Add corn and wine and cook until wine is reduced by half, about 5 minutes. Add clam juice, water, half-and-half, and saffron. Add lemon juice and whisk with a metal whisk (to prevent the half-and-half from curdling). Season broth with Tabasco and additional salt and pepper if needed. Add fish, potatoes, bacon, and parsley and simmer until fish and potatoes are heated through, about 5 minutes.

✓

Sweet Pea Soup

GRÖNÄRTSSOPPA SERVES 4–6

To keep this sweet and delicious soup bright green, cook the peas for a few minutes only and add lemon juice just before serving.

1 tablespoon butter
1 tablespoon olive oil
1 small onion, peeled and chopped fine
½ pound russet potatoes (1 small), peeled and chopped
2 cups chicken or vegetable broth
½ pound frozen sweet peas
juice of 1 lemon (3 tablespoons)
salt and pepper to taste

In a small stockpot, combine butter, olive oil, onion, and potatoes. Cook over low to medium heat, stirring often, until onion is translucent and potatoes begin to soften but before they turn brown, about 6–8 minutes. Season with salt and pepper. Add broth and cook until potatoes are fork tender, about 10 minutes. Add peas and immediately remove from heat. Using an immersion blender (or a conventional blender), process soup until smooth. Return soup to pot and season with lemon juice and additional salt and pepper to taste.

Wild-Mushroom Soup

SVAMPSOPPA SERVES 4–6

Wild mushrooms—chanterelles, porcini, and morels—grow abundantly in the Swedish forest. Swedes love hunting for wild mushrooms, and many take classes to help them recognize what is edible and what is not. Unless you are experienced in picking wild mushrooms, it is best to buy them at a farmer's market or from your grocer.

Assorted wild mushrooms are prepared simply for this savory soup recipe. But in Sweden, mushrooms frequently find their way into sauces that go with everything—from reindeer meat (page 39) to salmon to hot sandwiches (page 100)—or into a filling for Swedish pancakes (page 120).

1 small onion, peeled and chopped
¾ pound russet potatoes (1 medium), peeled and chopped
2 tablespoons butter
1 tablespoon olive oil
¾ pound assorted wild mushrooms (2 cups), brushed clean and sliced
3 ½ cups chicken or vegetable broth
½ cup half-and-half (optional)
1 tablespoon balsamic vinegar
salt and pepper to taste
1 small bunch chives, chopped

In a medium pot, combine onion, potatoes, butter, and olive oil. Cook until onion is translucent and potatoes begin to soften but before they brown, about 6–8 minutes. Add mushrooms and cook 3 minutes more. Season with salt and pepper to taste. Add broth and simmer for 10 minutes. Using an immersion blender (or a conventional blender), process soup briefly, leaving some of it chunky. Stir in half-and-half if desired. Season with balsamic vinegar and add salt and pepper if needed. Garnish with chives.

NOTES

NOTES

Potatoes

Potatoes are serious business in the very north of Sweden where I grew up, and without a doubt the world's best potatoes are grown there. Every family grows their own. Even apartment dwellers like my grandmother had access to a government-sponsored community plot, where she could be found way past her ninetieth birthday tending our tiny potato patch.

The most popular local variety is *mandelpotatis* (also known as Swedish Peanut), which is similar to a fingerling potato but denser, creamier, and full of starch. The deep yellow potato has skin so thin you hardly know it is there.

For the summer potato festival, which celebrates the glory of the midnight sun, a small batch of baby potatoes is gently dug, minutes before being served. Handled like fragile eggs, they are carefully scrubbed and then plunged into boiling salted water for just a few minutes. The potatoes are eaten piping hot, dipped first into a ramekin of melted sweet butter with fresh herbs, then into a small dish of sea salt and black pepper.

The rest of the crop is left in the ground until late fall, when it is harvested, washed, dried, and stored. The *mandelpotatis* skin becomes tougher the longer the potato is stored, while the potato itself becomes heavy in starch—making it an excellent wintertime ingredient for Swedish potato dumplings (page 10).

Baby New Potatoes with Sea Salt and Dill

POTATIS MED ÖRTER OCH SALT SERVES 4

Glorious baby new potatoes make me want to stand up and dance to the music of ABBA. *Mamma mia,* they are good! Use only the freshest, tiniest potatoes for this recipe.

1 cup unsalted butter (2 sticks), clarified
2 quarts water, salted
2 pounds baby new potatoes (about 25–30), such as Swedish Peanut,
   fingerling, Yukon gold, Peruvian blue, or red russet
4 tablespoons assorted fresh herbs, such as dill, chervil, chives, or rosemary, chopped fine
4 tablespoons sea salt, preferably fleur de sel
4 teaspoons coarsely ground black pepper

To clarify butter, melt it in a small, heavy saucepan over low heat. Remove from heat and let sit for a few minutes. With a spoon, remove and discard the foamy fat from the butter's surface. Spoon clarified butter into a small bowl for serving. Discard solids that remain on the bottom.

In a large saucepan, bring salted water to a boil. Add potatoes and cook until just soft, about 3–5 minutes. Drain into a colander and let dry on paper towels.

While potatoes are cooking, add herbs to clarified butter and divide equally into four ramekins. Serve potatoes on small plates with 1 tablespoon of salt and 1 teaspoon of black pepper on each and with the herb/butter mixture on the side.

Grilled Baby New Potato Salad with French Green Beans and Mint

POTATISSALLAD MED HARICOTS VERTS SERVES 4

Potatoes in all their glorious forms are served with almost every meal in Sweden. My mother still does not believe any meal is complete without potatoes. When she comes to visit I serve them with everything, including angel-hair pasta (with baby new potatoes, green beans, and cherry tomatoes) and risotto (with potatoes and wild mushrooms). This makes her feel as though she is getting a "real" meal.

This simple potato salad is beautiful, and when served with chicken or fish it is the perfect complement to a great summer meal. Add angel-hair pasta cooked al dente and tossed with olive oil, salt, and pepper, and you will have a great variation of pasta salad to satisfy any potato-loving Swede.

2 quarts water, salted
2 pounds baby new potatoes (about 25–30), assorted varieties and colors
    such as Peruvian blue, Russian fingerling, or Red Bliss
1 pound thin French green beans, ends cut off
olive oil spray
1 clove garlic, peeled and minced
1 tablespoon Dijon mustard
1 tablespoon balsamic vinegar
½ cup fresh flat-leaf parsley, chopped
1 tablespoon fresh mint, chopped
3 tablespoons extra-virgin olive oil
salt and pepper to taste
1 cup pitted, herbed kalamata olives (optional)
1 pint cherry tomatoes, halved (optional)

In a large saucepan, bring salted water to a boil. Add potatoes and cook until just soft, about 3–5 minutes. Drain into a colander and let dry on paper towels.

While potatoes are boiling, bring a small pot of water to a boil. Cook green beans until just done but still crisp, about 4–5 minutes. Drain immediately and rinse in cold water to stop cooking. Set aside on a small plate.

Light an outdoor grill or a stovetop grill pan. Cut cooked potatoes in half or, if they are tiny, leave whole. Spray cut side with olive oil, and grill cut side down until grill marks appear.

While potatoes are grilling, prepare the dressing. Mix garlic, mustard, vinegar, parsley, and mint in a small bowl. Slowly whisk in olive oil. When potatoes are grilled and still hot, toss them in the olive oil mixture and season with salt and pepper to taste. Add green beans and the olives and tomatoes if desired. Serve at room temperature.

Layered Three-Cheese Russet and Sweet Potato Gratin

POTATISGRATÄNG SERVES 6–8

The first time I tasted a potato gratin was at Petite Maxine, the French bistro in Luleå where I worked. Biting into the silky, buttery-smooth potato dish was an unforgettable moment because it was the instant I knew that food and cooking would always be my first love, and that the potato would be the star in this lifelong love affair.

The bistro's potato gratin was made with baking potatoes, garlic, cream, and—believe it or not—Kraft American cheese, which seemed sweeter and silkier than any Swedish cheese. This recipe mixes baking and sweet potatoes to create two distinct colored layers, and uses orange juice and chipotle peppers as seasonings.

2 tablespoons butter, divided
2 pounds baking potatoes (2 large), such as russet, peeled and sliced $\frac{1}{8}$-inch thin
3 cloves garlic, peeled and grated
fresh ground nutmeg to taste
3 teaspoons fresh thyme, minced fine
1 pound sweet potato (1 large), peeled and sliced $\frac{1}{8}$-inch thin
3 tablespoons orange juice concentrate, thawed
1 tablespoon adobo sauce from canned chipotle peppers
1 cup cheese, such as Gruyère, mozzarella, or Parmesan, or any combination, freshly grated
1 $\frac{1}{2}$ cups heavy cream
salt and pepper to taste

Preheat oven to 400 degrees Fahrenheit. Rub bottom of a 9 x 13-inch glass baking dish with 1 tablespoon butter. Add a third of the russet potatoes and season with salt and pepper to taste. Top with a third of the garlic and a small sprinkling of nutmeg and thyme. Add a third of the sweet potatoes, season with salt and pepper, and brush with 1 tablespoon of orange juice concentrate and a third of the adobo sauce. Spread a third of the cheese on top and add a third of the cream. Repeat twice, creating three layers of potatoes, each ending with the cheese and cream. Dot top layer with remaining butter. Bake until potatoes are fork-tender, crisp, and golden on top, about 45–60 minutes. Cover dish with aluminum foil if the top begins to burn.

Potato Salad with Herb Vinaigrette, Olives, and Red Onions

POTATISSALLAD MED OLIVER **SERVES 4**

This simple potato salad is lemony and tangy. Served with a sandwich for lunch or grilled chicken or fish for dinner, it makes a refreshing meal.

2 quarts water, salted
2 pounds (about 25–30) baby new potatoes
¼ cup fresh lemon juice
1 tablespoon white wine vinegar
1 clove garlic, peeled and minced
1 tablespoon Dijon mustard
¼ cup extra-virgin olive oil
½ cup assorted fresh herbs or greens, such as parsley, cilantro,
*   radicchio, chives, mint, or chervil, chopped*
½ cup pitted kalamata olives, chopped
¼ cup red onion, peeled and chopped fine

In a large saucepan, bring salted water to a boil. Add potatoes and cook until just soft, about 3–5 minutes. Drain into a colander and let dry on paper towels.

While potatoes are cooking, prepare dressing. Mix lemon juice, vinegar, garlic, and mustard in a small bowl. Slowly whisk in olive oil. Cut potatoes into halves or quarters (depending on size) and transfer to a bowl. Stir in herbs, olives, and onion. Toss dressing with potatoes while they are still warm. Let marinate for at least 30 minutes before serving.

Tricolored Potato Hash with Bacon, Corn, and Roasted Red Pepper

PYTT I PANNA SERVES 6–8

Pytt i panna translates to all good things "put in the pan"—potatoes, onion, and leftover meats all chopped fine and sautéed until golden brown.

Although this favorite Swedish dish is equally satisfying if you use leftover vegetables and cold cuts, this recipe includes three kinds of potatoes (or, if you prefer, use russet potatoes only), plus bacon, corn, and red peppers. You may also substitute gravlax (page 61) or smoked salmon for the bacon; just add the salmon at the same time you add the roasted red peppers. Serve the hash for breakfast with an egg fried sunny side up and pickled beets (page 86) or as a light lunch with a simple green salad.

Pytt i panna made with finely cubed steak (such as filet mignon) and served with a raw egg yolk in the center is called *biff à la Rydberg*.

6 slices bacon, preferably apple-wood smoked, sliced thin crosswise
3 tablespoons butter, divided
3 tablespoons olive oil, divided
1 pound russet potatoes (1 large), peeled and diced into ¼-inch pieces
¾ pound sweet potatoes (1 medium), peeled and diced into ¼-inch pieces
½ pound Peruvian blue potatoes (3 small), peeled and diced into ¼-inch pieces
salt and pepper to taste
1 medium onion, peeled and diced fine
1 cup fresh or frozen corn
1 red pepper, roasted and chopped fine
½ cup fresh flat-leaf parsley, chopped

In a large skillet over high heat, cook bacon until crisp. Drain on paper towels and set aside. In a clean skillet heat 1 tablespoon butter and 1 tablespoon olive oil. Add the russet potatoes and cook, while stirring, until lightly browned and cooked through, about 2–3 minutes. Transfer potatoes into bowl. Repeat steps with sweet potatoes and Peruvian blue potatoes. Combine all potatoes in bowl, season with salt and pepper, and cover to keep warm.

Cook onion in the skillet until translucent, about 3–4 minutes, and season lightly with salt and pepper. Add corn and cook for 3 minutes more.

To roast peppers, char them over an open flame or under a broiler; peel off blackened skins. Add peppers to onion and corn, then add bacon and potatoes. Stir to combine and sprinkle with parsley.

Jansson's Temptation with Smoked Salmon and Capers

JANSSONS FRESTELSE **SERVES 4–6**

Jansson's Temptation is a rich, delectable concoction of potatoes, onions, anchovies, and cream. It is the star dish of the Swedish smörgåsbord, the lox, cream cheese, and bagel of Swedish cuisine. This recipe is made with the more readily available gravlax (page 61) or smoked salmon. If Swedish anchovies are available at a specialty store near you, use them if you wish.

Potatoes, salty fish, and cream pose the ultimate temptation to forgo the diet and indulge. Consider the fall of Erik Jansson, a Lutheran pietist who spent a lifetime rejecting all personal indulgences until he encountered this powerfully aromatic dish. He fell from grace when he was caught with a mouthwatering forkful by a shocked disciple. It was the beginning of the end of religious fanaticism in Sweden.

16 ounces gravlax (page 61) or smoked salmon
¼ cup fresh dill, chopped fine
2 tablespoons capers, drained and rinsed
1 medium onion, peeled and chopped fine
3 pounds russet potatoes (6 medium), peeled and sliced julienne
zest and juice of 1 lemon (3 tablespoons)
¾ cup crème fraîche or sour cream
1 ½ cups heavy cream
4 tablespoons cornflake crumbs or regular dry bread crumbs
4 tablespoons butter, cut into small pieces

Preheat oven to 400 degrees Fahrenheit. Butter a 9 x 13-inch glass baking dish. Spread salmon, dill, capers, and onion in the bottom of the dish. Toss potatoes with lemon zest and lemon juice and season with salt and pepper. In a small bowl, whisk together crème fraîche or sour cream and cream, stir into the potato mixture, and cover salmon with potatoes. Sprinkle with cornflake or bread crumbs and scatter small pieces of butter on top. Cover with aluminum foil and bake for 25 minutes; remove foil and bake uncovered until potatoes are tender and top is browned, about 20 minutes more.

Skillet-Roasted Potatoes with Fresh Herbs and Lemon

RÅSTEKT POTATIS MED ÖRTER OCH CITRON SERVES 4–6

I experienced a lot of food firsts at the French bistro in Luleå, like potato gratin and potatoes cooked in goose fat. Goose fat gives potatoes a rich flavor and turns them golden brown and crunchy like French fries. Goose fat is usually available at well-stocked gourmet markets, but olive oil is a good substitute. Served with whole roasted chicken (page 56) and a simple green salad, it is cooking at its best.

2 tablespoons goose fat or olive oil
2 pounds baby new potatoes (about 16–20), peeled and halved
1 garlic clove, peeled and minced
zest of 1 lemon
2 tablespoons fresh flat-leaf parsley, chopped
salt and coarsely ground black pepper

In a large skillet, cook goose fat over medium heat until hot. Add potatoes (first making sure they are completely dry, or the oil will splatter) and cook one side until just brown, about 5–6 minutes. Turn and brown the other side until soft on the inside and crisp on the outside, about 3–5 minutes more. Remove potatoes from the pan and place in a bowl. Stir in garlic, lemon zest, and parsley, and season with salt and pepper. Serve immediately.

Hasselback's Potatoes

HASSELBACKSPOTATIS SERVES 4–6

Traditionally, Hasselback's potatoes are brushed with butter only and sprinkled with bread crumbs, salt, and pepper, then baked. In this version, garlic, lemon, and parsley enhance the classic recipe.

3 pounds russet baking potatoes (about 6 medium), peeled
6 garlic cloves, peeled
½ cup olive oil, or enough to cover garlic cloves
1 cup dry bread crumbs
zest of 1 lemon
3 sprigs fresh flat-leaf parsley, chopped
1 tablespoon butter
juice of 1 lemon (3 tablespoons)
salt and pepper

Preheat oven to 350 degrees Fahrenheit. Cut thin, cross-length slices three-quarters of the way into each potato, an eighth of an inch apart (or as close as you can), being careful not to cut all the way through. Place potatoes in a bowl of cold water to prevent discoloring; set aside.

To prepare the topping, in a small saucepan heat olive oil over low heat, add garlic, and simmer until garlic is soft, about 15–20 minutes. Drain garlic and reserve oil in a separate bowl. In a small bowl, combine garlic, bread crumbs, lemon zest, parsley, butter, and salt and pepper. Remove potatoes from water and pat dry with paper towels.

In a small baking dish, place potatoes cut side up. Divide bread-crumb mixture evenly over potatoes, pressing the filling gently into the cuts. Bake until potatoes are soft and browned on top, about 45 minutes. If the topping starts to burn before potatoes are done, cover loosely with aluminum foil.

While potatoes are baking, prepare the vinaigrette. Whisk 2 tablespoons of reserved olive oil into lemon juice and season with salt and pepper. Spoon a small amount of the lemon vinaigrette onto each potato.

Potato Pancakes

RÅRIVNA POTATISPLÄTTAR SERVES 4-6

In Scandinavia there are as many different potato pancake recipes as varieties of potatoes. The pancakes may be made using this recipe, with eggs, flour, and cream. For a softer pancake, replace the 2 tablespoons of cream with 1 cup milk. You may also omit both eggs and cream, creating a pancake that is similar to a latke (held together by the flour). The pancakes can be made tiny, as appetizers garnished with sour cream and gravlax, or larger for breakfast with bacon, sour cream, and lingonberries (page 178). Either way, crispy potato pancakes are simple and quick to make and a real crowd-pleaser.

1 ½ pounds russet baking potatoes (2 medium), peeled and shredded coarse
1 medium yellow onion, peeled and shredded coarse
1 tablespoon lemon juice
½ cup flour
2 eggs
2 tablespoons heavy cream
¼ cup vegetable oil
salt and pepper

Place potatoes and onion in cheesecloth and squeeze out the liquid. Transfer mixture to a medium-size bowl and toss with lemon juice to prevent discoloring. In a small bowl, whisk the flour, eggs, and cream and stir into the potato mixture. In a large skillet, heat oil until hot but not smoking. Depending on size of pancake desired, spoon ¼ cup (more or less) of the potato mixture into the pan and flatten slightly with a spatula. Cook a few potato pancakes at a time, without crowding the pan, until all the batter is used. Let each pancake cook until golden and crisp, about 2–3 minutes, before turning and cooking on the opposite side for 1–2 minutes more. Drain on paper towels, transfer to a sheet pan or serving platter, and season with salt and pepper on both sides.

Classic Mashed Potatoes

POTATISMOS SERVES 4

Potatoes, butter, and cream—life does not get much better. *Food* does not get much better.

6 cloves garlic, peeled
½ cup olive oil, or enough to cover garlic cloves
2 pounds russet baking potatoes (4 medium), peeled and chopped
½ cup butter (1 stick), cut into small pieces
1 cup heavy cream
salt and coarsely ground black pepper
white pepper

Preheat oven to 300 degrees Fahrenheit. Place garlic in a small glass baking dish and pour enough olive oil on top to immerse the cloves. Cover with aluminum foil and bake until soft and golden brown, about 30 minutes. Drain garlic; reserve oil for other use or discard. In a large stockpot, boil potatoes in salted water until fork-tender, about 10–15 minutes. Drain in colander and return potatoes to the pot. Cook on medium high heat, while stirring, for a few minutes to evaporate any excess water. Remove from heat and press potatoes through a ricer (optional). Transfer potatoes to a mixing bowl and whip potatoes on medium speed using the whisk attachment. Add garlic and butter in batches. Add cream and season to taste with salt, black pepper, and white pepper.

Potatoes Cooked in Cream and Dill

DILLSTUVAD POTATIS **SERVES 4**

Potatoes cooked in dill are usually eaten with smoked fish or gravlax. The traditional recipe uses only baking potatoes, milk, and dill. This recipe is made with three kinds of potatoes, fresh herbs, and rich, garlic-infused heavy cream. If you prefer, use only russet potatoes.

¾ pound russet potatoes (1 medium), peeled and cut into ½-inch cubes
¾ pound sweet potatoes (1 medium), peeled and cut into ½-inch cubes
½ pound Peruvian blue potatoes (2 small), peeled and cut into ½-inch cubes
6 cloves garlic, peeled
2 cups heavy cream
1 cup assorted fresh herbs, such as dill, parsley, or chives, chopped
salt and pepper

In a medium saucepan, cook potatoes in salted water until they just begin to soften, about 5 minutes. Do not overcook potatoes or they will become too soft and break when stirred into the cream. Drain water and return potatoes to pan.

While the potatoes are cooking, place garlic in a small saucepan, cover with water, and simmer 3 minutes. Drain water and repeat (this process removes any bitterness from the garlic). Add cream to garlic and cook until garlic is very soft, about 15 minutes. Mash garlic into cream. Add cream to potatoes and cook 3 minutes more or until potatoes are hot. Add herbs and season with salt and pepper to taste.

Vegetarian Potato Lasagna

POTATISLASAGNE SERVES 4–6

Because my mother does not believe that pasta is real food, I have replaced the pasta sheets in this classic lasagna recipe with thin sheets of potatoes, creating a hearty dish that no Swede can complain about. If you prefer, use a marinara sauce with meat or turkey.

2 cups water, salted
3 cups baby spinach (5 ¼-ounce bag), washed
2 cups whole-milk ricotta cheese (15-ounce container)
1 bunch fresh flat-leaf parsley, chopped
zest from 1 lemon
½ cup Parmesan cheese, freshly grated, divided
2 pounds russet potatoes (2 large), peeled and cut into rectangular blocks
1 tablespoon butter
2 cups marinara sauce, homemade or purchased
salt and pepper

Preheat oven to 400 degrees Fahrenheit. In a medium saucepan bring salted water to a boil. Add spinach and cook for 1 minute. Drain and rinse under cold running water. Squeeze out excess water, chop the spinach, and stir into ricotta cheese. Add parsley, lemon zest, and 1 tablespoon of Parmesan into spinach mixture. Season lightly with salt and pepper.

With a mandoline or a sharp knife, cut potatoes lengthwise into ¼-inch-thick slices. In a large pot of salted water, boil potato sheets until they begin to soften but before they become too soft to easily handle, about 5 minutes. Rub butter on bottom of 8 x 10-inch glass baking pan. Add a layer of potatoes to the pan, trimming slices to fit if necessary. Sprinkle lightly with salt and pepper, spread on a thin layer of marinara sauce, then spread on half the ricotta cheese mixture. Repeat layers, ending with potatoes and a thin, final layer of marinara sauce, sprinkled with Parmesan. Bake uncovered for 20 minutes, then cover with aluminum foil and bake until potatoes are cooked through, about 10–20 minutes more. Let rest for 10 minutes before carving into slices.

NOTES

NOTES

Meat, Game, and Chicken

Every summer, we traveled about two hundred miles in our 1968 white VW bug from Luleå to visit relatives near the small village of Stensele in the heart of Lapland. The highway soon gave way to smaller and smaller roads. Two hours into the trip, the roads were no longer paved and hundreds of acres of forest surrounded us. Then, from nowhere, they appeared: a sea of reindeer, crossing the road in front of our tiny car. All we could do was turn off our engine and wait. The deer will not stop for you; you stop for them. Hundreds streamed past the car at a slow and steady pace, never taking notice of us, just heading their way. Ten minutes, fifteen minutes—time stood still until, just like that, they were gone. They vanished into the forest as quickly as they had appeared. As we restarted the engine and resumed our journey, we were alone in the forest once more.

Other times, while I was picking lingonberries and cloudberries deep in the forest with my grandmother, an elk would suddenly stroll by as I sat under underneath the branches of a giant pine. All I heard was the snapping of twigs as the animal walked past with its graceful, gliding steps. The peace of the forest, the sweetness of the berries, and the majesty of the elk captivated me.

Consumption of elk meat is customary in Sweden, as is eating the meat of reindeer, which are herded and owned by the Sami people. Reindeer meat is found in all Swedish markets, usually sold frozen and sliced very thin.

To prepare reindeer meat, Swedes sauté it in butter with onions and wild mushrooms, then add heavy cream and chopped parsley. Enjoyed with boiled potatoes and lingonberry preserve (page 178), it would be a delicacy anywhere in the world. Because wild game is not readily available or necessarily desirable in American markets, I have based most recipes in this section on chicken or more popular meats, using spices and techniques from Swedish wild-game recipes.

Absolut Wild Game with Chanterelle Mushrooms

ÄLGSTEK MED KANTARELLSÅS SERVES 6

1 leg of venison, boneless and trimmed
1 large carrot, peeled and chopped
1 medium onion, peeled and chopped
1 celery stalk, chopped
4 cloves garlic, peeled
2 bay leaves
½ bottle red wine
¼ cup vodka, preferably Absolut
salt and pepper to taste
olive oil spray

Mushroom Sauce:
oil for cooking
2 cups chicken broth
1 cup heavy cream
3 tablespoons butter
2 tablespoons shallots, chopped fine
3 cups assorted wild mushrooms, such as morels, chanterelles, and porcini
1 tablespoon fresh lemon juice
1 tablespoon flour
1 teaspoon Worcestershire sauce
1 bunch fresh chives, chopped
salt and pepper to taste

Place venison in a large baking dish and evenly divide carrots, onion, celery, garlic, and bay leaves. Pour wine and vodka over venison and vegetables and let marinate, turning once, in refrigerator overnight.

Preheat outdoor grill and preheat oven to 450 degrees Fahrenheit. Remove venison from marinade and pat dry, reserving marinade to make the sauce. Salt and pepper venison generously on all sides, then spray meat on all sides with olive oil spray (or brush on a thin layer of oil). Grill over high heat on each side until seared and browned, about 5 minutes. Place on a baking sheet and bake 30 minutes, then reduce oven temperature to 350 degrees and continue baking until the meat's internal temperature reaches 150 degrees, about 15 minutes more. Remove venison from the oven and let rest for 15 minutes.

While venison is cooking, prepare the sauce. Remove vegetables from the reserved marinade with a slotted spoon. In a medium sauté pan, in a small amount of oil, combine carrots, onion, and celery and cook until they begin to soften, about 5 minutes. Pour marinade over vegetables and boil until reduced to about ½ cup. Strain through a fine mesh strainer; discard solids. Return reduced wine to pan and add broth. Cook sauce about 10–15 minutes to reduce by half, add cream, and cook 5 minutes more.

While venison is resting, melt butter in a medium sauté pan and cook shallots until translucent, about 2–3 minutes. Add mushrooms and cook 5 minutes more. Season with salt, pepper, and lemon juice, then sprinkle flour over the mixture. Pour wine sauce over mushrooms. Simmer 5 minutes and season with Worcestershire sauce, chives, and additional salt and pepper if needed.

Carve venison into thin slices. Arrange on platter. Pour mushroom sauce around the meat.

Roasted Rack of Venison with Herb Vinaigrette

RENKOTLETTER MED BASILIKASÅS **SERVES 4–6**

It is considered a duty and a community service to help reduce the elk population in the north of Sweden. Hunting elk prevents car accidents, which are much too common as the animals bolt into fast-moving highway traffic. So every August my uncle and other men of my mother's generation would gather their weapons and wander into the forest to hunt for elk. We would eagerly wait for my uncle to bring home the fresh game. The choice cuts would be eaten right away, simply seasoned and grilled. Leaner and tougher cuts would be frozen to last us through the long winter months.

olive oil spray
3 racks of venison (4 chops to each 1 pound rack), Frenched (trimmed between bones)
1 lemon, quartered and grilled
3 cloves garlic, peeled
1 tablespoon lemon zest
½ cup fresh flat-leaf parsley, chopped
3 tablespoons olive oil

Herb Vinaigrette:
1 cup fresh basil, chopped
½ cup spinach, chopped
¼ cup extra-virgin olive oil
1 tablespoon balsamic vinegar
1 clove garlic, peeled and minced

Preheat an outdoor grill. Spray venison on all sides with olive oil spray (or brush on a thin layer of oil). Grill venison over high heat until seared and browned, about 2 minutes on each side. Grill lemon quarters until browned, about 2 minutes per side. Season venison with salt and pepper and place on a baking sheet. In a small bowl, combine garlic, lemon zest, parsley, and olive oil, rub over the meat, and season generously on all sides with salt and pepper. Let marinate at room temperature for 20 minutes.

To prepare the vinaigrette, combine basil, spinach, olive oil, vinegar, and garlic in a blender (or food processor); blend until smooth. Season with salt and pepper.

Preheat oven to 400 degrees Fahrenheit. Bake venison until meat thermometer registers desired doneness (120 degrees for rare, 125 for medium rare), about 10–25 minutes. Remove from oven and let rest 10 minutes before carving. Garnish with grilled lemon, which can also be used to season the meat, and serve with herb vinaigrette.

Beef Tenderloin with Sweet Corn Sauce

FILET MIGNON MED MAJSSÅS SERVES 6–8

Anytime there is a reason to celebrate in Sweden, you just need a toast (skål!) and a roast. Beef tenderloin is a savory, easy-to-prepare roast that is moist, tender, and appropriate for any special occasion. For a larger crowd, it is easier and more elegant to cook a whole filet.

Because we were a small family, my grandmother, my mother, and I would eat individual filet mignon steaks with morel sauce (page 40) on birthdays and holidays. To cook individual filets, use ¾-inch thick (5-ounce) filets seasoned generously on both sides with salt and pepper. Cook over high heat in a skillet on each side until well browned and the desired doneness.

olive oil spray
1 whole beef tenderloin (2 ½ pounds), skin and fat removed
2 garlic cloves, peeled and minced
2 tablespoons olive oil
1 sprig fresh rosemary, minced
salt and pepper

Sweet Corn Sauce:
1 small onion, peeled and chopped
2 tablespoons butter
1 cup fresh sweet corn (not frozen or canned), cut from 2 medium ears
½ cup chicken (or vegetable) broth
½ cup water
1 tablespoon fresh chives, minced
1 black truffle, sliced thin (optional)

Preheat outdoor grill or stovetop grill pan. Spray tenderloin on all sides with olive oil spray (or brush on a thin layer of oil). Grill on all sides until well browned, about 7–8 minutes. Transfer to a baking sheet.

Preheat oven to 400 degrees Fahrenheit. In a small bowl combine garlic, olive oil, and rosemary. Rub over tenderloin and season generously with salt and pepper. Bake until desired doneness: 10–15 minutes for rare (120 degrees), 15–20 minutes for medium (130 degrees), or 25 minutes for well done (140 degrees). Let rest for 20 minutes before carving.

While beef is roasting, prepare the sauce. In a small saucepan, cook onion in butter until translucent but not browned, about 5–8 minutes. Add corn, broth, and water; bring to a boil for 5 minutes. Using an immersion blender (or a conventional blender), process the corn mixture until smooth. Strain through a fine mesh strainer; discard the solids. Season corn mixture with salt and pepper and stir in chives. Add truffles to sauce if desired. Carve roast to desired thickness and arrange on serving platter. Serve sauce hot with carved tenderloin.

Juniper- and Lavender-Marinated Rack of Lamb

MARINERADE LAMMKOTLETTER **SERVES 4–6**

Lamb is usually the main course for Easter Sunday, with halibut (page 71) the customary entrée for Good Friday. A great cut of meat, simply prepared and served with fresh potatoes and spicy yogurt (below), makes a hard-to-resist country meal.

olive oil spray
2 racks of lamb (1 ½ pounds each), Frenched (trimmed between bones)
2 tablespoons olive oil
1 clove garlic, peeled and minced
1 tablespoon lemon zest
1 sprig fresh organic lavender, minced fine
1 tablespoon juniper berries, crushed
salt and pepper

Lemon and Roasted Jalapeño Pepper Yogurt:
1 cup plain yogurt or kefir
juice of 1 lemon (3 tablespoons)
2 sprigs fresh mint, minced fine
½ cup cucumber, preferably European seedless, sliced julienne
1 jalapeño pepper, roasted, peeled, seeded, and minced

Preheat outdoor grill or stovetop grill pan. Spray lamb on all sides with olive oil spray (or brush on a thin layer of oil). Grill until browned, about two minutes per side. Transfer to baking sheet or roasting pan.

Preheat oven to 400 degrees Fahrenheit. In a small bowl, combine olive oil, garlic, lemon zest, lavender, and juniper berries. Rub mixture over lamb and season generously on all sides with salt and pepper. Bake until desired doneness: 5–10 minutes for rare (120 degrees), 10–15 minutes for medium (130 degrees), or 20 minutes for well done (140 degrees). Let rest 10–15 minutes before carving.

To make seasoned yogurt, combine all ingredients in a small bowl. Let yogurt sit for a minimum of 30 minutes before serving.

Calf's Liver with Bacon and Caramelized Onion

LEVER STEKT I SKIVOR MED LÖK OCH BACON **SERVES 4–6**

Calf's liver and pig's feet are two Swedish delicacies my grandmother seemed to make on a weekly basis, but I have seldom encountered them here in America. She would spend hours at the stove, stirring the flavorful pig's feet as our apartment slowly filled with the scent of tender pork. Pig's feet are traditionally served as part of an elaborate Christmas buffet (page xxi) and are considered a delicacy. After being cooked for hours to soften, they are then soaked in a salt brine for half a day and enjoyed cold with pickled beets (page 86).

I was never a huge fan of pig's feet. The flavor is delicious, but I could not quite take to the texture. But when my grandmother cooked calf's liver, I was first at the table to enjoy the smooth, silky texture. Serve liver with potatoes and lingonberries (page 178). If liver is not your favorite cut, substitute thin turkey breast cutlets.

4 slices bacon, preferably apple-wood smoked, cut crosswise into ½-inch pieces
1 small red onion, peeled and sliced into thin wedges
2 tablespoons butter, divided
2 tablespoons olive oil, divided
2 Bosc pears, peeled, cored, and sliced into wedges
1 tablespoon balsamic vinegar
4–6 slices calf's liver, ½ inch thick each
salt and pepper
4 tablespoons flour
fresh parsley, chopped (to garnish)

In a medium skillet, cook bacon over high heat until crisp. Drain on paper towels and set aside. In the bacon fat cook onion over medium heat until translucent, about 2–3 minutes. Add 1 tablespoon butter, 1 tablespoon olive oil, and pears to the pan and cook until soft and lightly browned, about 3–5 minutes. Sprinkle with vinegar and cook 1–2 minutes more. Transfer cooked pear-onion mixture to a bowl and cover with aluminum foil to keep warm.

Season calf's liver with salt and pepper and dredge each slice in the flour until lightly coated. Wipe the pan clean or use a new skillet, and melt the remaining butter and olive oil. Cook liver until browned, about 3–4 minutes per side. Transfer to serving platter, adding pear-onion mixture and bacon on top. Garnish with parsley.

Roasted Garlic and Sun-Dried Tomato Stuffed Loin of Pork

FLÄSKFILÉ MED VITLÖK   SERVES 4–6

All things rich, divine, and extravagant are eaten on Fat Tuesday, the day before Lent begins. This was a practical matter in the past, when churchgoers prepared for the lean days of Lent to follow. This is the day that semlor (Fat Tuesday buns, page 131), my favorite Swedish specialty dessert, is served, preceded by a loin of pork or other rich meat dish. The pork for Fat Tuesday is usually stuffed with dried prunes or apricots (or both) and served with baked brown beans seasoned with sugar, maple syrup, and vinegar. In this recipe, the pork is filled with roasted garlic and sun-dried tomatoes. Serve with white bean salad (page 92) or traditional brown beans (page 93).

Pork is also served in a dish called *dopp i grytan* ("dip in the kettle") to celebrate the anticipation and arrival of Christmas. The family gathers around the stove, dipping freshly baked country bread (limpa with raisins, page 153) into bowls filled with the salty, flavorful broth used to cook the Christmas ham— or a separate broth made with pork, potatoes, and carrots.

1 loin of pork roast (3 ½ pounds), trimmed and ready to bake
12 oil-cured sun-dried tomatoes (1 cup), drained
6 cloves garlic, peeled and roasted (page 16)
1 cup fresh basil, chopped
3 tablespoons butter
2 tablespoons olive oil
1 carrot, peeled and chopped coarse
1 celery stalk, chopped coarse
1 small onion, peeled and chopped coarse
salt and pepper
1 cup chicken broth
1 cup orange juice
3 sprigs fresh parsley

Preheat oven to 350 degrees Fahrenheit. With a sharp knife, poke six holes (evenly divided along the length of the roast) into the center of the roast. Lay one sun-dried tomato on a cutting board, put a garlic clove in the center with 1 tablespoon of chopped basil, and cover with another tomato. Repeat with remaining tomatoes, garlic, and basil. Stuff each hole in the roast with 1 garlic-filled tomato, using the handle of a wooden spoon to widen the holes if necessary. In a large roasting pan, heat butter and olive oil. Add pork and brown on all sides over high heat. Add carrot, celery, and onion, and cook 2–3 minutes more. Season roast on all sides with salt and pepper.

In a small saucepan, combine broth, orange juice, and parsley. Let simmer until slightly reduced, about 5–8 minutes; discard parsley. Transfer roast to the oven and bake uncovered for 30 minutes. Turn roast over, add reduced juice/broth, and bake until meat thermometer registers 170 degrees, about 30 minutes more. Remove from oven, cover with aluminum foil or lid, and let rest 10–15 minutes. Remove roast from pan, carve into thin slices, and transfer to a serving platter. Strain juices from pan and pour a small amount over the roast.

Oven-Baked Veal Roast with Parsley Vinaigrette

KALVSTEK MED PERSILJESÅS SERVES 6

The delicate flavor and fine texture of veal have appealed to generations of Swedes. In the spirit of Swedish *husmanskost* (country-style home cooking), this recipe is simple and unfussy in its preparation. Because of its lack of natural fat, veal can be easily overcooked and become dry, so toward the end of the roasting time keep a close eye on its doneness.

1 veal shoulder roast (about 3 ½ pounds), cleaned and tied with butcher string
2 tablespoons butter
zest of 1 lemon
½ cup fresh flat-leaf parsley, chopped coarse
2 cloves garlic, minced
salt and pepper
1 cup chicken broth

Parsley Vinaigrette:
½ cup fresh flat-leaf parsley, chopped coarse
2 cloves garlic, peeled and minced
⅛ cup capers, rinsed and drained
1 tablespoon shallots, minced
¼ cup balsamic vinegar
salt and pepper
¼ cup extra-virgin olive oil

Preheat oven to 350 degrees Fahrenheit. Cut 8–10 slits ⅓-inch deep into the top of the roast. In a small bowl melt butter and combine with lemon zest, ½ cup parsley, and 2 garlic cloves. Rub over the roast and into the slits. Season with salt and pepper. Place veal in a roasting pan and pour broth into pan. Roast meat, basting occasionally, until meat thermometer registers an internal temperature of 170 degrees, about 1 hour. Transfer veal to a platter and let rest for 15 minutes.

While roast is baking, make the vinaigrette. In a food processor, combine ½ cup parsley with garlic, capers, shallots, and vinegar. Season with salt and pepper and process 1 minute. While processor is running, add olive oil in a slow stream until incorporated.

Carve the veal into thin slices and serve with parsley vinaigrette.

Swedish Meatballs with Gravy

KÖTTBULLAR SERVES 4–6

In Sweden, less is usually more. But when it comes to meatballs, more is more. Swedish meatballs are much smaller and lighter than their Italian counterparts, so they are eaten by the dozen. There are many variations on Swedish meatballs and everyone has a favorite recipe they believe is best. What cannot be disputed is that it is one of the most famous dishes to come out of Sweden. *Everyone* has heard of Swedish meatballs (and *svenska flickor*—Swedish girls)!

Meatballs are made with many combinations of meats. Some cooks prefer ground beef only, while others use ground beef and pork, turkey, or veal. In general, all Swedish meatballs include bread crumbs and cooked onion and they are beaten until thoroughly blended. Although the meatballs are traditionally served with a cream-based gravy, they remain light and luscious. They can also be served with a marinara sauce. Either way, they are great with boiled or mashed potatoes (page 33) and lingonberries (page 178).

4 tablespoons butter, divided
2 tablespoons yellow onion, minced
2 slices soft white bread, torn into large chunks
2 cups chicken or beef broth, divided
1 ½ pounds mixed ground meats (such as ½ pound ground beef,
    ½ pound ground pork, and ½ pound ground turkey)
1 slice bacon, minced (optional)
½ teaspoon sugar
1 teaspoon salt
½ teaspoon pepper
1 tablespoon flour
½ cup heavy cream
olive oil
salt and pepper

In a large skillet, melt 1 tablespoon butter over medium heat and cook minced onion until translucent, about 1–2 minutes. Season with salt and pepper.

In a food processor, process bread until it turns into soft, fine crumbs. Add 1 cup broth, meats, bacon, sugar, 1 teaspoon salt, and ½ teaspoon pepper. Process 2–3 minutes or until thoroughly blended. Add cooked onion and blend 1 minute more. Put a small amount of olive oil on hands (or use wet hands) and form mixture into tiny (1 inch or smaller) balls. In a large skillet, melt 2 tablespoons butter over medium heat. When butter begins to foam, add meatballs. Stir and shake the pan until meatballs are uniformly browned on all sides and cooked through. Place meatballs on serving platter and cover with aluminum foil to keep warm.

To prepare the sauce, melt the remaining tablespoon of butter in the same skillet. Whisk in flour and, while stirring, cook until flour is incorporated into the butter and begins to lightly brown, about 30 seconds. Stir in remaining cup of broth and cook while whisking until the sauce begins to thicken, about 5 minutes. Add cream and cook 2–3 minutes more. Season gravy lightly with salt and pepper. Pour over meatballs and serve hot.

Chicken with Prosciutto and Gruyère Cheese with Apple-Pomegranate Relish

KYCKLINGRULADER MED OST, SKINKA OCH ÄPPELCHUTNEY SERVES 4–6

A Swedish favorite, *falukorv* is a lightly smoked, thick (two to three inches in diameter), boiled sausage, similar to ring bologna. It is sliced on sandwiches, sautéed with potatoes, oven-baked, and added to *pytt i panna* (page 28), but my favorite way of preparing *falukorv* is to stuff it with mustard, cheese, and apples before baking. Across a six-inch or longer length of sausage make several slits about three-fourths through. Place the sausage in a baking pan, spread mustard into each slit, and insert a slice of cheese or a wedge of apple. Bake until the sausage is browned, the cheese is bubbly, and the apple is soft. Cut into individual slices and serve.

This chicken recipe uses cheese, mustard, and apples to re-create the flavors of this classic sausage dish.

6 small chicken breast pieces, pounded between 2 sheets of
plastic food wrap to an even thickness of ¼ inch
3 tablespoons whole-grain Dijon mustard
6 thin slices prosciutto
6 thin slices Gruyère cheese
1 cup baby spinach (4 ounces)
salt and pepper
3 tablespoons butter
1 tablespoon olive oil

Apple-Pomegranate Relish:
1 tablespoon butter
1 large green apple, peeled, cored, and chopped fine
2 tablespoons sugar
1 tablespoon fresh lemon juice
¼ cup golden raisins
½ cup pomegranate seeds (optional)
½ cup walnuts, chopped coarse and toasted
1 tablespoon maple syrup

Place pounded chicken on cutting board, shiny side down. Spread a thin layer of mustard on chicken and layer 1 slice prosciutto, 1 slice Gruyère, and 2–3 spinach leaves on top. Roll chicken breast to enclose the filling, and fasten with toothpick (or tie with kitchen string) if necessary. Repeat with remaining breasts. Season prepared rolls with salt and pepper.

To make apple-pomegranate relish: In a small skillet, melt butter. Add apples and sugar and cook over medium heat until browned and soft, about 5–8 minutes. Add lemon juice, raisins, pomegranate seeds, walnuts, and syrup and heat 1 minute more. Remove from heat and keep relish warm until serving.

In a large skillet melt remaining butter and olive oil and cook chicken rolls over medium-high heat, turning occasionally until browned on all sides and cooked through. Cut into thin crosswise slices and serve with apple-pomegranate relish.

Rosemary Chicken Skewers with Bacon-Wrapped Figs

ROSMARINMARINERADE KYCKLINGSPETT MED FIKON SERVES 4–6

These chicken skewers may be served as a main course with baby new potatoes and a green salad. If the chicken is cut into smaller bites and baby figs are used, the skewers can be served as appetizers. If fresh figs are not available, omit them and wrap the bacon directly around the chicken pieces.

4 chicken breasts, skinned, boned, and cut into bite-sized cubes
2 cloves garlic, peeled and minced
¼ cup olive oil
2 sprigs fresh rosemary, chopped
zest and juice of 1 lemon (3 tablespoons)
1 teaspoon red hot-pepper flakes
salt and pepper
8 slices bacon, preferably apple-wood smoked
16 small fresh figs (or 4–8 larger figs cut in halves or quarters)

Place chicken in glass baking dish (or large zippered plastic food bag). In a small bowl, whisk garlic, olive oil, rosemary, lemon zest and juice, pepper flakes, and salt and pepper to taste. Pour marinade over chicken and marinate 30 minutes at room temperature or up to 4 hours in the refrigerator.

Preheat outdoor grill. Cut each bacon strip in half and wrap each fig with half a slice of bacon. Onto each metal skewer (or wooden skewers soaked in water to prevent burning), alternately place three pieces of chicken with two bacon-wrapped figs. Place skewers on hot grill (or stovetop grill pan) and grill until chicken is cooked through and bacon is crisp, about 5 minutes per side.

Chickenschnitzel with Caper Berries, Parsley, and Lemon

KYCKLINGSCHNITZEL SERVES 4

Chicken is not as popular in Sweden as it is in the United States. When I go home I find that most restaurants offer fish, typically salmon, and several meat dishes, but seldom chicken. This tangy, tart, and sumptuous chicken recipe uses the popular Swedish seasoning combination of lemon and kefir or buttermilk. Serve with classic mashed potatoes (page 33) and a dandelion greens salad (page 87).

4 skinless, boneless chicken breasts, pounded between 2 sheets of
*   plastic food wrap to an even thickness of ¼ inch*
salt and pepper to taste
1 cup buttermilk or plain original kefir or milk
1 egg
zest and juice of 1 lemon (3 tablespoons)
1 cup all-purpose flour
2 cups plain bread crumbs or cornflake crumbs
2 tablespoons butter
1 tablespoon olive oil
1 lemon, sliced thin
½ cup caper berries or ¼ cup regular capers, drained and rinsed
½ bunch fresh flat-leaf parsley, chopped

Season both sides of chicken breasts with salt and pepper to taste. In a bowl whisk buttermilk, egg, and lemon juice and zest. Put flour on one plate and bread crumbs on another. Dredge chicken first in flour on both sides, then dip into buttermilk and coat chicken in bread crumbs. Repeat with all chicken breasts. In a large sauté pan, combine butter and olive oil. When hot, add chicken and sauté on both sides over medium heat until brown, crisp, and cooked through, about 3–4 minutes per side. Drain on paper towels. Transfer to a serving platter and garnish with lemon slices, caper berries, and parsley.

Pineapple-, Orange-, and Lime-Marinated Chicken Breast

ANANASMARINERAD KYCKLING SERVES 8

On those rare occasions when chicken is served in Sweden, it is often presented in wild and strange combinations, such as in *flygande Jakobs gryta* ("flying Jacob's stew"), in which chicken, bananas, heavy cream, bacon, chili sauce, and peanuts are baked together. Try instead this simple three-citrus-marinade chicken recipe.

8 small chicken breasts, pounded between 2 sheets of
    plastic food wrap to an even thickness of ½ inch
6 tablespoons frozen pineapple juice concentrate, thawed
1 cup fresh orange juice
½ cup fresh lemon or lime juice
¼ cup extra-virgin olive oil
2 cloves garlic, peeled and minced fine
1 cup assorted herbs, such as parsley, cilantro, mint, rosemary, tarragon, or thyme, chopped
1 teaspoon hot red-pepper flakes
olive oil spray
salt and pepper to taste

Pineapple Salsa:
1 can (15 ounces) sliced pineapple in juice (not syrup)
3 tablespoons brown sugar
juice of 1 lime (2 tablespoons)
1 jalapeño pepper, seeded and chopped fine
2 tablespoons fresh cilantro, chopped

In a large glass baking dish (or in a zippered large plastic food bag), mix pineapple, orange, and lemon juices with olive oil, garlic, herbs, and pepper flakes. Toss chicken with marinade and marinate in the refrigerator a minimum of 2 hours or overnight.

While the chicken is marinating, make the pineapple salsa. In a small saucepan combine pineapple (with juice from the can) and brown sugar. Cook over low heat until sugar dissolves, about 3–5 minutes. Using an immersion blender (or a conventional blender), process pineapple until smooth and stir in lime juice, jalapeño, and cilantro.

Heat an outdoor grill on high, and spray grill surface with olive oil spray. Remove chicken from marinade and spray it on all sides with olive oil spray (or brush on a thin layer of oil). Grill chicken until cooked through and grill marks appear. Season with salt and pepper to taste. Serve with pineapple salsa.

Roasted Chicken with Root Vegetables

KYCKLING I UGN SERVES 4

I had never seen a large roasting chicken or a turkey before I came to America. Like most things in Sweden, chickens are smaller but more flavorful than their American counterparts. Swedish portions are much smaller as well. Meals consist of a small plate of simple, fresh, delicious food, eaten always with a knife and fork—even pizza! There are no supersized, handheld meals in the land of the Vikings. Of course, meals can never be so large that there is no room afterward for fika (page xxiii), which usually follows all meals.

Small roasted chickens in Sweden are typically seasoned with spices such as cinnamon, cardamom, and cloves. This recipe calls for a simple seasoning of lemon and garlic.

1 whole roasting chicken, rinsed and patted dry, giblets discarded
1 whole lemon, zest removed
6 cloves garlic, peeled
olive oil spray plus 3 tablespoons olive oil
½ teaspoon paprika
3 whole carrots, peeled and chopped
3 celery stalks, chopped
1 large onion, peeled and chopped
1 red bell pepper, stemmed, seeded, and chopped
¼ cup fresh flat-leaf parsley, chopped
salt and coarsely ground black pepper

Preheat oven to 475 degrees Fahrenheit. Place chicken in a roasting pan. Place the lemon (reserving zest) and 5 garlic cloves inside the chicken. Spray chicken on all sides with olive oil spray (or brush on a thin layer of oil). Season skin generously with salt, coarse black pepper, and paprika.

In a separate baking dish scatter carrots, celery, onion, and red pepper. Toss vegetables with 3 tablespoons olive oil and season with salt and pepper. Place chicken and vegetables in the oven and bake 30 minutes. Turn vegetables over, reduce heat to 375 degrees, and bake 30 minutes more, or until meat thermometer inserted into the thickest part of the chicken thigh registers 175 degrees or the juices run clear, about 30 minutes more.

While the chicken is baking, mince remaining garlic clove and combine with parsley and reserved lemon zest in a small bowl.

Remove chicken from oven and let rest for 5 minutes before carving. Stir garlic-lemon mixture into the vegetables and season with salt and pepper.

NOTES

Fish and Shellfish

A large percentage of Swedish families—nearly a quarter of the population—have summer homes. These tiny cottages are not owned just by the wealthy; even working families, apartment dwellers like we were, have little red-and-white getaways. Our summerhouse was a two-hour drive from Luleå, deep in the forest by the edge of a large, beautiful lake. My grandfather built the home, one log at a time, in the early 1920s.

Almost a century later, his grandchildren and their families still gather each summer at this tiny retreat. When I grew up, our cottage did not have electricity, which meant we did not have a refrigerator. We had only a cool storage—a deep hole in the ground, cemented in and covered with a heavy lid, where we could keep perishable foods from spoiling for a few days. But mostly we ate what we caught or picked each day—fish from the lake, potatoes from the little garden, berries from the forest. We ate the freshest foods available out of necessity. We were fishermen; we were hunters and gatherers. We all helped provide.

Once summer arrives, and it is light all evening long, the Swedes stay outdoors as much as possible. Early in the morning, with the sun already high, my uncle and all the children would pile into our small boat and slowly row to the center of the glimmering lake and wait quietly for fish to bite. My cousins and I would compete to see who would catch the biggest fish of the day. Whether we brought home pike, zander, or perch—the most bountiful (and bony) fish in the lake—we were always proud to eat our own catch. Nothing tasted better.

Other times, we rose at dawn, driving to go fishing in the large, wild rivers nearby, where we would catch succulent, tender salmon that we grilled and ate that same day. Any salmon we could not eat immediately we would make into gravlax, with its tasty marinade of salt, sugar, and fresh dill (page 61), and savor at a later time.

No matter what the weather, we tried to eat all our summer meals outside. Battling mosquitoes, the most feared beast of the Swedish forest, we would set up the table with grilled fish stuffed with fresh dill, seared lemon wedges, and sea salt and serve baby potatoes and a cucumber or dandelion greens salad on the side. Each meal was a glorious celebration of summer, with the adults lifting their glasses in skål every other minute. With each skål, the feared mosquitoes seemed not so bothersome after all.

Once a summer we would have a crayfish party (*kräftor*, page 78), one last outdoor skål before the end of the season. These amazing freshwater shellfish—similar to lobster, but much smaller—are boiled and seasoned with dill and enjoyed while drinking satisfying quantities of vodka, schnapps, and beer.

Aquavit and Dill-Marinated Salmon

GRAVLAX   SERVES 10–12

Gravlax is a famous Swedish specialty that is surprisingly simple to prepare—much easier to make than smoked salmon. Salt, sugar, dill, and forty-eight hours will turn fresh salmon into this translucent, paper-thin delicacy. Some cooks like the sugar-to-salt ratio of gravlax to be split fifty/fifty, while others use two parts salt to one part sugar. Either way it is delicious.

Gravlax can be served on any occasion, whether a country breakfast or a wedding celebration. It is served on sandwiches with dill sauce (page 62), as a garnish on a spectacular sandwich cake (*smörgåstårta*, page 105), or with potato pancakes (page 32). It is even eaten cooked, as a substitute for herring in *Janssons frestelse* (Jansson's Temptation, page 29) or in *pytt i panna* (page 28).

Gravlax will keep tightly wrapped in plastic food wrap for two weeks in the refrigerator or for months in the freezer.

2 salmon fillets (each 12 inches long, 4–6 inches wide, and at least 1 inch thick), skin on
½ cup to 1 cup kosher salt (or any coarse salt)
½ cup to 1 cup sugar
2 bunches fresh dill
1 tablespoon aquavit or cognac (optional)

Inspect salmon for bones, using a tweezers to gently remove. In a small bowl mix salt and sugar. *The amount of salt and sugar depends on the size of the salmon: 5 pounds of fillets will need about ¾ cup each of salt and sugar.* Prepare a piece of aluminum foil longer than the fillets. Rub skin side of one fillet with a thin but thorough coating of salt/sugar mix. Place skin side down on the foil and sprinkle flesh side with the salt/sugar mix in a thin but even layer. Spread fillet with dill and sprinkle with aquavit, if desired. Place second fillet flesh side down over the first. Sprinkle with remaining salt/sugar mix (or, depending on size of fillets, spread the mix in a thin, even layer). Wrap salmon tightly in aluminum foil, then wrap it again in plastic food wrap to form an airtight pocket. Place in a dish (to catch any escaping juices) and put a cutting board or other lightweight object on top to compress salmon slightly. Refrigerate 48 hours, turning the salmon over every 12 hours.

After salmon has marinated, separate the fillets, discard the dill, and rinse off the salt/sugar mix under cold running water. Pat dry with paper towels. With a sharp knife cut the fillets diagonally into the thinnest slices possible, the same way smoked salmon is sliced. While cutting, detach each slice from the skin; discard the skin. Garnish gravlax with fresh dill and lemon slices.

Gravlax with Mustard-Dill Sauce and Fresh Baby Spinach

GRAVLAX MED DILLSÅS SERVES 4–6

Gravlax is traditionally served with mustard-dill sauce and boiled, peeled potatoes. The sauce also goes well with grilled salmon, whether left whole or cut into fillets (page 64–65).

18 thin slices gravlax (or 3 slices per person) (page 61)

Mustard-Dill Sauce:
3 tablespoons Dijon mustard
juice of 1 lemon (3 tablespoons)
1 tablespoon honey
¼ teaspoon coarsely ground black pepper
salt to taste
⅓ cup vegetable oil
2 tablespoons fresh dill, minced

Baby Spinach:
1 tablespoon olive oil
18 small baby new potatoes, boiled and quartered
4 cups baby spinach leaves
1 cup cherry tomatoes, halved
4 hard-boiled eggs, chopped coarse

To make mustard-dill sauce, combine mustard, lemon, honey, pepper, and salt in a bowl or food processor and process for 1 minute. With the motor running, slowly add the vegetable oil to make a smooth, thick sauce. Stir in dill.

To make the spinach, heat the olive oil in a large skillet. Add potatoes and cook until browned and crispy. Season with salt and pepper to taste. Remove from heat and stir in spinach and tomatoes.

Place spinach-potato mixture on a serving platter, drizzle with mustard-dill sauce, and garnish with gravlax and hard-boiled eggs.

Smoked-Salmon Tartar

GRAVLAX TARTAR SERVES 4 (AS AN APPETIZER)

Smoked-salmon tartar can be served as a filling for a sandwich cake (page 103) or as is with boiled potatoes. It can also be served on halved hard-boiled quail eggs as an elegant appetizer or on potato chips.

To make fresh potato chips, peel russet baking potatoes and slice with a mandoline on a very thin
setting ($1/16$ inch). Place slices in a bowl with cold water and 1 tablespoon sea salt and let sit for 1 hour.
Rinse slices well and pat dry. Fry potato slices in vegetable oil over moderate heat until golden. Drain
chips on paper towels and sprinkle with salt and pepper to taste.

8 ounces gravlax (page 61) or smoked salmon, minced
4 tablespoons red onion, minced
½ cucumber, preferably European seedless, minced
2 tablespoons capers, drained and rinsed
2 tablespoons fresh dill, minced
1 tablespoon fresh lemon juice
2 tablespoons mayonnaise

Combine all ingredients in a small bowl.

Grilled Salmon Fillets with Tarragon and Pink-Peppercorn Sauce
GRILLAD LAX MED ROSÉPEPPARSÅS SERVES 4–6

Salmon is the most popular fish in Sweden, whether eaten as gravlax or cooked fresh with a variety of sauces. Grilled salmon is often served with a cold sauce of whitefish roe (page 68). This recipe uses a classic tarragon and pink-peppercorn sauce.

6 small salmon fillets (4–5 ounces each), skinned and boned
2 tablespoons coarse salt
olive oil spray (or 1–2 tablespoons olive oil)

Pink-Peppercorn Sauce:
2 cups white wine
1 shallot, peeled and minced
1 cup heavy cream
salt and pepper
3 tablespoons butter
1 tablespoon fresh tarragon, minced
1 tablespoon pink peppercorns

Place salmon in a small glass dish and sprinkle lightly with salt. Marinate 2 hours in the refrigerator. Preheat outdoor grill or stovetop grill pan. Rinse salmon under cold running water to remove salt and pat dry with paper towels. Spray or brush with olive oil. Grill salmon, flesh side down first, over medium heat until grill marks appear, about 4–5 minutes. Turn and grill salmon on skin side until cooked through, about 3–4 minutes more.

While salmon is marinating, prepare the sauce. In a small, heavy saucepan, combine wine and shallot and cook over medium-high heat until reduced to a few tablespoons, about 10 minutes. Add cream and cook until sauce has thickened slightly, about 5–8 minutes more; season lightly with salt and pepper. Remove from heat and whisk in butter, tarragon, and pink peppercorns. Keep whisking until butter is melted and incorporated. Keep sauce in a warm place until serving.

Grilled Salmon Fillets with Herb Butter and Cucumber Salsa

GRILLAD LAX MED GURKSALSA SERVES 8

Fermented Baltic herring (*surströmming*) is eaten in the summer only. You have to smell this foul delicacy to believe it; in all my travels and food adventures, I have never encountered anything edible that has as obscene an odor. It is banned in apartment buildings because its pungent fumes can permeate the entire complex in seconds, sending residents scampering for relief.

Fermented Baltic herring is served in a ceremonial outdoor feast with boiled potatoes, *wasa* crisp bread, an array of regional cheeses, pickled vegetables, and a platter of lettuce, cucumber, and tomatoes. Eating it the first time is sort of an initiation into adulthood. Afterward, you feel as if you have joined a club of Vikings from times past.

For the uninitiated (and less brave), Swedish salmon is the way to go. Salmon is beautiful to look at, sweet smelling, and appealing to everyone. Herb butter makes this grilled salmon moist and flavorful. Because fresh vegetables are not often available in the north of Sweden, salmon is often served with a side of pickled cucumbers (page 85). Here, the crisp coolness of cucumber salsa is an excellent accompaniment to the salmon's creaminess.

8 small salmon fillets (4–5 ounces each), skinned and boned
olive oil spray
salt and pepper to taste
⅓ cup fresh orange juice, plus zest of 1 orange
⅓ cup fresh lemon juice, plus zest of 1 lemon
⅓ cup fresh lime juice, plus zest of 1 lime
¼ cup extra-virgin olive oil
1 cup assorted fresh herbs, such as parsley, basil, arugula, rosemary, dill, and tarragon, chopped
1 clove garlic, peeled and minced
8 tablespoons butter

Cucumber Salsa:
½ cucumber, preferably European seedless, minced
1 Roma tomato, cored, seeded, and minced
½ onion, peeled and minced
1 tablespoon chopped fresh arugula, dandelion greens, or parsley
juice of 1 lemon (3 tablespoons)
1 teaspoon jalapeño pepper, minced

To make cucumber salsa, combine all ingredients and let marinate for at least 1 hour before serving.

Preheat oven to 400 degrees Fahrenheit. Preheat outdoor grill or stovetop grill pan. Spray flesh side of salmon fillets with olive oil (or brush lightly with oil). Grill fillets top side down until grill marks appear, about 2–3 minutes. Transfer fillets to a baking sheet, grilled side up. Season with salt and pepper, and pour orange, lemon, and lime juices on top. Drizzle with $\frac{1}{4}$ cup olive oil and sprinkle fillets with $\frac{1}{4}$ cup of the herb mixture. With a food processor (or by hand in a bowl), blend zests and remaining herbs with garlic and butter until a paste forms. Shape into log and wrap in plastic food wrap.

Bake fillets until translucent, about 10–12 minutes depending on size. Remove from oven and add a small dollop of herb butter on each fillet. Serve with cucumber salsa.

Oven-Baked Whole Salmon with Dill, Rosemary, and Lemon

LAX MED ROSMARIN OCH CITRON SERVES 8–10

A whole baked salmon brought to the table is a simple but spectacular dish. It is often served as part of a Christmas Eve buffet, but it is as great for a casual family meal as it is for special celebrations. Serve the fish with lemon wedges only or with mustard-dill sauce (page 62) or cucumber salsa (page 65), and on the side include baby new potatoes (page 24).

1 whole salmon (6–8 pounds), scaled and gills and bones removed
salt and pepper
6 tablespoons butter
1 clove garlic, peeled and minced fine
1 cup assorted fresh herbs, such as dill, rosemary, chervil, parsley, chopped fine
zest and juice of 1 lemon (3 tablespoons)
¼ teaspoon hot red-pepper flakes

Preheat oven to 400 degrees Fahrenheit. Rinse salmon well under cold running water and pat dry with paper towels. With a sharp knife, cut decorative crisscross marks on top of salmon, deep enough to go through the skin only. Season salmon inside and out with salt and pepper.

In a food processor or a small bowl, combine butter, garlic, herbs, lemon juice and zest, and pepper flakes until well blended. Smear three-quarters of the butter mix inside the salmon and spread the rest into the cuts on top of the fish. Place salmon in a baking dish or on a rimmed baking sheet, cover loosely with aluminum foil, and bake until a meat thermometer registers 135 degrees, about 30–40 minutes.

Marinated Arctic Char with Whitefish Roe Sauce

With its beautiful pink-dotted skin and rose-colored flesh, it is easy to see how arctic char is related to both salmon and trout. Arctic char thrives in the icy cold waters off the north coast of Sweden, although it is also farm-raised and readily available at most well-stocked fish markets.

¼ cup sugar
⅛ cup salt
1 tablespoon coarsely ground white pepper
4 arctic char fillets (6 ounces each), skin on
½ cup fresh dill, chopped

Whitefish Roe Sauce:
1 cup crème fraîche (or sour cream)
8 ounces golden whitefish roe (American golden, löjrom, page 111)
2 tablespoons fresh dill, chopped
juice of 1 lemon (3 tablespoons)
salt and pepper (optional)
sunflower sprouts (optional)

In a small bowl, combine sugar, salt, and white pepper. Rub a small amount on both sides of char fillets. Sprinkle with dill and marinate overnight in the refrigerator. Rinse fillets under cold running water and pat dry with paper towels. In a large, nonstick skillet, sear the fillets, skin side down first, until crispy, about 3–4 minutes. Carefully, without breaking skin of fish, use a rubber spatula to turn the fillets over and cook opposite side until just cooked through, about 3 minutes more. Do not over-cook as fish easily becomes dry. Transfer to a serving platter.

To make the sauce: combine crème fraîche, roe, dill, and lemon juice. Season lightly with salt and pepper if desired. Serve fish on a bed of sunflower sprouts (optional).

Grilled Fish Kebabs with Tomato Salad

FISKSPETT MED TOMATSALLAD SERVES 4–6

Make these quick and easy fish kebabs for a delicious and casual outdoor barbecue. Fresh, great-tasting fish needs very little seasoning.

3 fish steaks such as halibut, swordfish, or salmon (6–8 ounces each and 1 inch thick)
½ cup extra-virgin olive oil
3 cloves garlic, peeled and sliced thin
fresh rosemary sprigs
1 lemon, cut into small wedges
10 fresh (or dry) bay leaves
salt and pepper
olive oil spray

Tomato Salad:
3 vine-ripened tomatoes, cored, peeled, and chopped coarse
1 clove garlic, peeled and sliced thin
1 tablespoon olive oil
1 tablespoon balsamic vinegar
2 tablespoons basil, sliced julienne
2 tablespoons capers, rinsed and drained
2 cups croutons, purchased or freshly made (page 11)
salt and pepper to taste

Preheat outdoor charcoal or gas grill. Cut fish into cubes and place in glass dish. Pour oil on top and add garlic and rosemary. Marinate for 1 hour, turning once. Using metal skewers, make kebabs by alternating fish, lemon, and bay leaf. Season each kebab with salt and pepper. Spray grill with olive oil to prevent fish from sticking. Grill kebabs on each side until just done, about 3–4 minutes.

To make tomato salad: In a medium bowl, combine tomatoes, garlic, olive oil, vinegar, basil, capers, and croutons. Season with salt and pepper.

Cabbage-Wrapped Sea Bass with Saffron Sauce

FISKKÅLDOLMAR **SERVES 4–6**

Kåldolmar—ground pork and seasoned rice wrapped in cabbage, sautéed, and served with potatoes—is a classic Swedish dish in the spirit of *husmanskost* (page 48). In this recipe, the cabbage is gently steamed to maintain its translucent green color, then stuffed with fragrant sea bass.

To prepare the traditional dish, make a filling of 1 cup ground pork, 1 cup cooked rice, 2 tablespoons milk, and salt and pepper to taste. Enclose the filling in steamed cabbage leaves. Sauté the cabbage rolls in 2 tablespoons of butter until browned on each side. Add 3 cups water or chicken broth to the pan, cover, and simmer until the cabbage is soft and the filling is completely cooked, about 30 minutes.

3 quarts water
1 small head of cabbage (red, green, or collard greens, or a combination of all three),
    leaves gently separated to keep whole
6 fillets sea bass, halibut, or salmon (4–5 ounces each)
1 lime, cut into thin slices
2 Roma tomatoes, seeded and minced
2 cloves garlic, peeled and sliced thin
½ cup fresh flat-leaf parsley, minced

Saffron Sauce:
1 cup mayonnaise
2 cloves garlic, peeled and minced
1 pinch saffron threads, soaked in 1 tablespoon warm water
2 tablespoons lemon juice

In a large pot bring 3 quarts of water to a boil over high heat. Add cabbage leaves and cook until they begin to soften, about 2–3 minutes. Drain leaves and rinse under cold running water. Pat dry with paper towels. Place a large cabbage leaf on a cutting board, place a fish fillet in the center, and top with 1 slice of lime, 1 tablespoon minced tomato, a few slices of garlic, and 1 teaspoon parsley. Season with salt and pepper to taste. Wrap cabbage leaf tight around the fish, trim excess leaf, and secure with toothpick if needed. Repeat with remaining fillets. Place cabbage-wrapped fish inside a steamer, cover, and steam over high heat until fish is done, about 10 minutes.

To make saffron sauce, stir together mayonnaise, garlic, saffron, and lemon juice (plus water from soaking saffron threads) in a small bowl.

Transfer cabbage-wrapped fish to platter and serve with saffron sauce.

Halibut with Fresh Herb Crust

HÄLLEFLUNDRA MED ÖRTSKORPA SERVES 4

Fresh herbs are a celebration of spring's arrival. Although halibut is traditionally eaten on Good Friday in Sweden, it is delicious at any time of year. The beautiful, bright green herb crust in this recipe can be used on many types of fish fillets, including salmon and sea bass. It is best to use mild-flavored herbs as the fish can be easily overpowered by the stronger flavors of tarragon or rosemary, for example.

4 tablespoons butter, divided
1 tablespoon olive oil
4 small halibut, salmon, or sea bass fillets (4–5 ounces each), skinned
salt and pepper
3 slices white bread
1 cup assorted fresh herbs (such as dill, basil, parsley, chervil, and arugula)
zest of 1 lemon
½ teaspoon hot red-pepper flakes

Preheat oven to 400 degrees Fahrenheit. In a large skillet, melt 1 tablespoon butter with olive oil over medium-high heat. Sear fillets flesh side down for 2–3 minutes. Transfer fillets seared side up to a baking sheet, and season with salt and pepper. In a food processor, mix remaining 3 tablespoons of butter with bread, herbs, lemon zest, and pepper flakes, and blend until smooth. Evenly divide and spread the bread-crust mixture on the seared side of the fillets. Bake until opaque and herb crust begins to brown, about 10–12 minutes. Cover with aluminum foil if the crust begins to burn.

Fillet of Sole with Lemon Sauce and Baby Artichokes

FISK MED CITRON OCH KRONÄRTSKOCKA SERVES 4–6

Although we could not catch our own Dover sole when I was growing up, it is readily available fresh in Sweden. Many varieties of flatfish referred to as sole in the United States actually belong to the flounder family. True sole (the best known being Dover) is found only in European waters and is imported frozen to America. Any of the sole recipes in this book can be made with flounder as well. Sole is a delicately flavored fish with a fine, firm texture.

8 baby artichokes
6 fillets Dover sole or flounder (4–5 ounces each)
salt and pepper
½ cup all-purpose flour
6 tablespoons butter, divided
2 tablespoons olive oil, divided
2 Roma tomatoes, peeled, seeded, and minced
zest and juice of 1 large lemon (3 tablespoons)
2 tablespoons fresh herbs, such as parsley or chervil, chopped fine

Prepare artichokes by cutting off their stems at the base. Peel back and discard rough outer leaves. Cut off the top third (green tips) and cut tips in half. If artichokes are prepared ahead of time, place in a bowl of cold water with lemon juice.

Season fillets with salt and pepper, then dredge each side in flour and shake off excess. In a large skillet, melt 2 tablespoons butter over medium heat with 1 tablespoon olive oil. Cook fillets until browned and cooked through, about 2–4 minutes on each side. The flesh should begin to flake when done. Transfer to a platter and cover to keep warm.

Wipe skillet clean, add 1 tablespoon butter to remaining tablespoon of oil, and sauté artichokes until they begin to soften, about 5 minutes. Stir in remaining 4 tablespoons of butter, heat until it froths, then add tomatoes, lemon juice and zest, and herbs. Pour over fillets and serve at once.

Fillet of Sole with Leeks, Tomatoes, and Olives

FISK MED TOMATER OCH OLIVER SERVES 4

This easy dish can be prepared in the morning and placed in the oven just before serving. If you prefer a dairy-free recipe, omit the cream and the tomato paste. Pour the wine over the fish bundles and add the remaining ingredients.

2 tablespoons butter
1 large leek, white part only, sliced fine
salt and pepper
½ cup dill, chopped
8 Dover sole fillets (4–5 ounces each) or flounder (page 72)
1 cup white wine
1 ½ cups heavy cream
2 large ripe tomatoes, cored, seeded, and chopped into medium chunks
1 tablespoon tomato paste
1 cup pitted black kalamata olives
Tabasco sauce to taste
juice of 1 lemon or lime (3 tablespoons)

Preheat oven to 400 degrees. In a medium sauté pan, melt butter and cook leeks on low heat until opaque, about 3–5 minutes. Season with salt and pepper and stir in half the dill. Lay each fillet flat on a cutting board, and put a small tablespoon of cooked leek-dill mixture at the top (wide end) of the fillet. Roll fillet toward you, enclosing the mixture. Transfer fillet to a baking pan. Continue with remaining fillets, making two rows of four bundles each. Salt and pepper the bundles lightly.

In a small saucepan, cook and reduce the wine over medium heat until only a few tablespoons remain, about 5–8 minutes. Add cream and simmer over medium heat until sauce is slightly thickened, about 5–8 minutes more. Stir in tomatoes, tomato paste, olives, Tabasco, lemon or lime juice, and remaining dill. Season sauce with salt and pepper and pour over sole. Bake until fish easily flakes, about 12–15 minutes. Serve with boiled potatoes and a cucumber salad with mint and parsley.

Grilled Lake Trout with Lemon and Mint

GÄDDA MED CITRON SERVES 4–6

Midsummer's Day is celebrated June 24. After decorating the maypole with leaves and flowers, Swedes young and old put on their national costumes and dance around the maypole, singing traditional songs long into this night when the sun never sets. This is the beginning of summer, the beginning of new possibilities—the night when dreams come true. Traditionally, young girls (and boys) pick wildflowers and place them under their pillows in the hope they might dream of their future bride or groom.

I would skip past our tiny summerhouse and down to the meadow to gather a bouquet to tuck under my pillow. Every year I dreamed the same dream: I was walking through a green pasture, carrying a basket of fresh fruits and vegetables. But I was alone, not with my dream mate. The next morning my uncle would tease, "Did you dream of your lover? Did you meet your future groom in your dreams?" And off I would run, holding back the tears, because I thought my dream meant I would always be alone, carrying that sorry basket on my arm. Of course, the midsummer dreams of my childhood did come true, and food did become my first love. And I have since learned that when you have an overflowing basket of fresh fruits and vegetables, you will never be alone. Many will gather at your abundant table.

Our midsummer feast was eaten at the summerhouse. Freshly dug potatoes with butter and sea salt (page 24) took center stage along with flaky, tender fish fresh from the lake and seasoned simply with herbs and lemon. Platters of gravlax with aquavit (page 61), zesty pickled cucumber salad (page 85), *wasa* bread (page 154), and assorted regional cheeses were also served. For dessert we would eat juicy ripe berries, freshly picked in the forest and served with sugar and whipped cream.

olive oil spray
6 whole trout (10–12 ounces each), cleaned and scaled
salt and pepper
½ cup fresh mint or dill, chopped
2 lemons, cut into quarters

Preheat an outdoor grill. Spray trout on both sides with olive oil (or rub lightly with olive oil). Season fish inside and out with salt and pepper and fill with mint or dill. Grill fish (either in a grilling basket or directly on the grill) over medium to high heat until just cooked through, about 5 minutes per side. Turn fish once only. Grill lemon quarters alongside the fish. Transfer fish and lemons to a serving platter. Squeeze half the lemon over the fish, reserving the other quarters as garnish. Sprinkle with additional mint or dill.

Cornflake-Crusted Crispy Fried Freshwater Perch

ABBORRE MED MAJSFLINGSKORPA SERVES 4–6

Perch can be tiny, offering little meat for all the work of eating around the many bones. But when you catch your own, and you have on your plate the biggest fish caught that day, the magic of summer makes this the best-tasting fish around.

6 whole freshwater perch, trout, or red snapper (10–12 ounces),
  cleaned and scaled with bones, heads, and tails removed
salt and pepper
½ cup all-purpose flour
1 cup cornflake crumbs (or regular bread crumbs)
2 eggs, beaten with 1 tablespoon milk
½ cup fresh dill
1 lemon, sliced very thin
4 tablespoons butter, divided
1 tablespoon olive oil

Preheat oven to 400 degrees Fahrenheit. Season fish inside and out with salt and pepper. Place flour and cornflake crumbs on separate plates; put eggs and milk in a large bowl. Dredge each fish in the flour, shake off excess, dip fish into egg mix, then coat with cornflake crumbs. Stuff each fish with a small amount of dill and 3 slices of lemon. (It is easier to stuff the fish after it has been coated because the filling tends to fall out during the process.) In a large skillet heat 2 tablespoons butter and olive oil until it begins to foam. Add fish, in batches if necessary, cooking until crisp, about 3–5 minutes per side. Transfer to oven and bake until fish is cooked through, about 5 minutes. Open each fillet slightly and place a small amount of butter inside (1 teaspoon for each fish from the remaining 2 tablespoons of butter). The butter will melt inside the hot fish.

Lake Trout Stuffed with Tomatoes and Garlic

ABBORRE MED TOMATER **SERVES 4**

Wild lake trout are found in cold-water lakes. They vary in size and can grow quite large and thus too oily. Large lake trout are best prepared smoked. For this recipe, use only small, freshly caught lake trout or farm-raised rainbow trout.

4 small whole trout (10–12 ounces each), cleaned and scaled, with heads and tails left on
salt and pepper
2 tomatoes, cored, seeded, and chopped
1 clove garlic, peeled and sliced thin
2 tablespoons olive oil
1 tablespoon basil, minced
2 eggs, lightly beaten
1 cup dried bread crumbs
1 cup all-purpose flour

Preheat oven to 400 degrees Fahrenheit. Rinse and dry trout, and season inside and out with salt and pepper.

In a small bowl, combine tomatoes, garlic, 2 tablespoons olive oil, and basil. Season lightly with salt and pepper. Whisk eggs in a small bowl and place bread crumbs and flour on separate plates. Dip each trout first into the flour, shaking off excess, then into eggs; coat last with bread crumbs. Stuff each fish with a small amount of tomato filling. (It is easier to stuff the fish after it has been coated because the filling tends to fall out during the process.) Put fish in a 9 x 13-inch buttered pan and bake uncovered until fish flakes, about 10-12 minutes.

Shrimp with Orange, Tomato, and Tabasco
RÄKOR MED APELSINSÅS **SERVES 4–6**

The tiny arctic shrimp is the most popular variety of shrimp in Sweden. However, arctic shrimp are always sold precooked and usually served in cold dishes such as shrimp sandwiches (page 107), so they are not suitable for this particular recipe.

One of my childhood friends, Monica, prepared this sweet and spicy shrimp dish for me during one of my recent visits to Sweden.

1 tablespoon butter
1 tablespoon olive oil
2 pounds raw jumbo or extra-large shrimp, peeled and deveined
salt and pepper

Orange, Tomato, and Tabasco Sauce:
1 tablespoon olive oil
1 small onion, peeled and diced
1 green pepper, diced
1 cup small button mushrooms, cleaned
3 tablespoons frozen orange juice concentrate, undiluted
½ cup heavy cream
1 can diced tomatoes (14 ½ ounces)
2 teaspoons liquid hot-pepper sauce (Tabasco sauce)
juice of 1 lime (2 tablespoons)
salt and pepper
½ cup assorted herbs, such as parsley, dill, chives, or basil, chopped

To make the sauce, in a small, heavy saucepan, combine onion, green pepper, mushrooms, and olive oil. Cook until onions are translucent, about 5–8 minutes. Add orange juice, cream, tomatoes, pepper sauce, and lime juice. Cook until sauce begins to thicken, about 5–6 minutes. Season with salt and pepper and stir in the herbs.

In a large skillet melt butter and olive oil over high heat until hot. Add shrimp and sauté until just pink, about 3–4 minutes, then season with salt and pepper. Stir cooked shrimp into sauce. Serve over a bed of cooked rice or boiled potatoes.

Crayfish Feast

KRÄFTOR   SERVES 4–6

Once a year in August, we gathered at my aunt and uncle's house for Sweden's traditional crayfish feast—one of the last outdoor celebrations before the long winter and the dark nights returned. The table would be set outdoors, rain or shine. My aunt had the complete crayfish setup: plates and platters with loud, showy crayfish designs, party hats and napkins with brightly colored crayfish patterns, a multitude of different size glasses for schnapps, vodka, and beer. There was no mistaking that the event's big deal was the tiny crustacean, prepared simply with dill, lemon, and butter, and served with freshly baked country bread, tender boiled baby new potatoes, and a platter of sliced regional cheeses.

The eating of crayfish is an art form and a ritual: eat only the tail and forgo the tiny legs and claws, and you will be ridiculed. A true Viking, a true Swede, uses toothpicks if necessary to remove the tiniest pieces of meat and finishes off each crayfish by sucking the salty and fragrant juices out of the head, followed by shouting "Skål!" before moving on to the next crayfish. By sundown, only scraps of shell and empty bottles of schnapps, vodka, and beer would be left, and another summer would have passed.

6 pounds live crayfish, rinsed (discard dead ones)
½ cup salt
½ cup sugar
large bunch of fresh dill
1 carrot, peeled and left whole
1 celery stalk
melted butter, clarified (page 24)
1 jalapeño pepper, sliced into very thin rounds (optional)
1 tablespoon fresh cilantro, minced (optional)
fresh dill (for garnish)
lemon wedges (for garnish)

In a large stockpot add enough water to cover the crayfish. Add salt, sugar, dill, carrot, and celery. Over high heat, bring water to boil and add the crayfish; cover and return to a boil. Reduce heat to a simmer and cook until crayfish have turned red, about 10 minutes. Drain the crayfish, discard the vegetables, and allow crayfish to cool.

Combine butter with jalapeño and cilantro if desired, and divide into individual dipping bowls. Transfer crayfish to a serving platter and garnish with additional dill and lemon wedges. Serve with clarified butter for dipping, crusty French bread, boiled potatoes, and a simple green salad.

TOP: *Trio of Swedish green soups. From the front: Potato and Leek Soup (page 14), Asparagus and Yukon Gold Potato Soup (page 13), Nettle, Sorrel, and Baby Spinach Soup (page 11).* **BOTTOM:** *Grilled Baby New Potato Salad with French Green Beans and Mint (page 25).*

TOP: *Roasted Rack of Venison with Herb Vinaigrette (page 42), with Tricolored Potato Hash with Bacon, Corn, and Roasted Red Pepper (page 28).* **BOTTOM:** *Halibut with Fresh Herb Crust (page 71), with Classic Mashed Potatoes (page 33) and micro beet greens.* **OPPOSITE:** *Swedish Pancakes (page 118) and Yellow Pea Soup with Bacon, Cherry Tomatoes, and Parsley (page 7).*

TOP: *Pineapple-, Orange-, and Lime-Marinated Chicken Breast (page 55), with steamed French green beans and Layered Three-Cheese Russet and Sweet Potato Gratin (page 26).*
BOTTOM: *Oven-Baked Swedish Bacon Pancake (page 116).* **OPPOSITE:** *Trio of Swedish salads. From the front: Dandelion Greens Salad with Gooseberries and Cilantro Vinaigrette (page 87), White Bean Salad with Roasted Red Peppers and Cherry Tomatoes (page 92), and Roasted Baby Beet Salad (page 86).*

TOP: *Marinated Arctic Char with Whitefish Roe Sauce (page 68), with sunflower sprouts.* **BOTTOM**: *A Fat Tuesday Bun (page 131).* **OPPOSITE**: *Cabbage-Wrapped Sea Bass with Saffron Sauce (page 70).*

TOP: *Saffron and Raisin Buns, known fondly in Sweden as Lussekatter buns (page 130)*. **BOTTOM**: *Chilled Rose Hips Soup topped with whipped cream (page 4)*.

NOTES

Vegetables
and Salads

Salads in Sweden are made mostly with cucumbers, carrots, beets, dandelion greens, cabbage, and grains or beans. The short summers do not allow much else to grow. My aunt had a small greenhouse in her yard, where a few precious tomatoes would ripen each year. She had more luck with cool-weather vegetables such as potatoes, carrots, beets, and cucumbers. She could also find dandelion greens growing wild at the side of the road. Most salads in this chapter are made using those ingredients.

My aunt also had great success growing a small plot of strawberries. As soon as I arrived at her house, I would slip into her strawberry patch to eat any ripe berries I could find. Few made it into the house; they were almost all consumed as we stood in the garden. They were tiny but sweet and delicious, more like the French *fraises des bois* than the large, mostly flavorless varieties found in the United States.

My aunt also grew rhubarb, and made many of her desserts by mixing the tangy, tart rhubarb with the sweet, mellow strawberries. Her little garden grew only a modest selection of regional fruits and vegetables, but it has given me a lifetime of memories.

Spring Green Beans with Anchovies, Tomatoes, and Olives

HARICOTS VERTS MED OLIVER SERVES 4–6

Use only thin French green beans—haricots verts—for this recipe. Cooked al dente and tossed with ripe red tomatoes and black olives, the beans can be used as a side dish for dinner or served as a salad with a sandwich.

4 cups thin French green beans (2 pounds), trimmed
2 canned anchovies, minced (optional)
1 clove garlic, peeled and minced
1 tablespoon fresh lemon juice
1 tablespoon balsamic vinegar
1 teaspoon Dijon mustard
salt and pepper
3 tablespoons extra-virgin olive oil
2 cups cherry tomatoes, halved
½ cup kalamata olives, pitted
½ cup dandelion greens, or other bittersweet greens such as arugula, chopped fine

In a medium-size pot, bring to a boil enough salted water to cover the beans. Add the beans and cook until just done but still crisp, about 4–5 minutes. Drain beans and plunge immediately into ice-cold water to stop the cooking. Drain on paper towels.

In a small bowl, combine anchovies, garlic, lemon juice, vinegar, and mustard. Season with salt and pepper. Slowly whisk in olive oil until combined. In a large bowl combine cooked green beans, tomatoes, olives, and dandelion greens. Mix with dressing and serve.

Variation

For a warm salad: Put salad in a baking dish and heat it in a 400 degree Fahrenheit oven for 5 minutes.

Celery Salad

SELLERISALLAD **SERVES 4**

The thin, crispy celery in this recipe goes well with the dressing's creaminess. The dressing is also terrific for Caesar salad.

3 stalks celery, tough outer strings removed and center section sliced julienne
1 cup cherry tomatoes (1 basket), halved
½ small red onion, peeled and sliced fine
½ cup croutons, purchased or homemade (page 11)

Dressing:
1 clove garlic, peeled and minced
juice of ½ lemon (1 ½ tablespoons)
1 tablespoon Parmesan cheese, grated
1 tablespoon Worcestershire sauce
1 tablespoon mayonnaise
salt and pepper
¼ cup olive oil

In a large bowl, combine celery, tomatoes, onion, and croutons.

To make dressing, combine garlic, lemon juice, Parmesan, Worcestershire sauce, mayonnaise, and salt and pepper in a small bowl. Slowly whisk in olive oil. Toss salad with dressing and serve.

White Asparagus Salad

SPARRISSALLAD SERVES 4

White asparagus is available in Sweden from May until midsummer. Europeans prefer the thick stalks and smooth texture of white asparagus to the more common green asparagus.

2 quarts water, salted
20 thick white asparagus stalks (2 bunches), peeled and rough ends cut off
olive oil spray or olive oil
1 red pepper, roasted and chopped fine
¼ cup feta cheese, crumbled
¼ cup pitted kalamata olives, chopped
½ cup fresh basil, sliced julienne

Dressing:
1 clove garlic, peeled and minced fine
2 tablespoons white-wine vinegar
3 tablespoons olive oil
salt and pepper

In a medium pot, bring to a boil 2 quarts of salted water, or enough water to cover asparagus. Add asparagus and cook until it is just done but still slightly crunchy, about 3–5 minutes depending on thickness of stalks. Drain and immediately plunge into ice-cold water to stop cooking. Drain on paper towels.

Spray asparagus with olive oil (or lightly coat with olive oil), and in a stovetop grill pan or on an outdoor grill, grill asparagus until seared, about 1–2 minutes per side. Lay cooked asparagus on a serving platter and scatter red peppers, feta cheese, olives, and basil on top.

In a small bowl, whisk garlic, vinegar, and olive oil. Season with salt and pepper. Pour over asparagus salad.

Lemongrass and Lime Cucumber Salad

GURKSALLAD SERVES 4–6

In Sweden, when you ask for a side of salad with your meal, the dish brought to you would most likely be a cucumber salad, with a few wedges of tomatoes on the side. This recipe spices up the original with the addition of lemongrass and hot chili peppers.

1 cucumber, preferably European seedless, sliced very thin
¼ cup red onion, peeled and sliced thin
¼ cup fresh cilantro, chopped
½ lime, sliced very thin
1 stalk lemongrass, light green center only, sliced thin
¼ cup white-wine vinegar
¼ cup sugar
1 teaspoon salt
¼ teaspoon red hot peppers

Place cucumber, onion, cilantro, and lime in a medium-size bowl. Combine lemongrass in a medium-heavy saucepan with vinegar, sugar, and salt. Cook over low heat for 3 minutes. Let cool, stir in red hot peppers, and pour over cucumbers. Marinate for a minimum of 1 hour before serving.

Roasted Baby Beet Salad

RÖDBETSSALLAD SERVES 4–6

Pickled beets are the most popular accompaniment to Swedish dishes. *Pytt i panna,* pig's feet, and many other dishes are served with beets. They also have a prominent place on the Swedish smörgåsbord.

This beet salad is delicious served with arugula or baby beet greens, mozzarella or goat cheese, and a sprinkling of walnuts.

3 cups assorted varieties baby beets, such as golden, Candy Cane, or baby red (2 pounds)
1 tablespoon olive oil
1 tablespoon red onion or shallot, chopped fine
2 tablespoons balsamic vinegar
2 tablespoons olive oil
1 tablespoon chives, chopped fine
salt and pepper to taste
1 tablespoon poppy seeds

Preheat oven to 400 degrees Fahrenheit. Mix beets and 1 tablespoon olive oil in a small baking pan. Cover with aluminum foil and bake until beets are fork-tender, about 1 hour. Let cool, then peel the beets. Slice beets thin (or chop them coarse). In a small bowl, combine beets, onion, vinegar, 2 table-spoons olive oil, and chives. Season with salt and pepper to taste. Garnish with poppy seeds. Marinate for a minimum of 1 hour before serving.

Dandelion Greens Salad with Gooseberries and Cilantro Vinaigrette

MASKROSSALLAD SERVES 4–6

Dandelion greens are weeds that grow both cultivated and wild. They grow in abundance by the sides of the roads in Sweden and are one of the few edible fresh greens available. Find them in your own garden or at most farmer's markets. Use only the freshest, youngest dandelion greens you can find, as the older leaves tend to be too bitter and slightly chewy. The bright green leaves can be easily replaced with arugula.

2 cups dandelion greens, chopped coarse
2 cups butter lettuce, chopped coarse
¼ cup radishes, sliced very thin
1 basket Sweet Cape gooseberries (1 cup), outer husks removed
2 ounces goat cheese, crumbled

Dressing:
1 small clove garlic, peeled and minced
2 tablespoons fresh lime juice
2 tablespoons fresh cilantro, chopped
salt and pepper to taste
4 tablespoons extra virgin olive oil

In a large bowl, combine dandelion greens and lettuce. Stir in radishes, gooseberries, and goat cheese.

To make the dressing, in a small bowl whisk garlic, lime juice, cilantro, and salt and pepper to taste. In a slow stream add olive oil and keep whisking until the dressing is emulsified. Toss salad ingredients with dressing and season with additional salt and pepper if desired.

Dandelion Greens with Bosc Pears and Shallots

KOKTA MASKROSOR MED PÄRON **SERVES 4**

The sweetness of pears combined with the tanginess of dandelion greens is a winning combination. Cooking the greens mellows their bitterness.

1 tablespoon butter
1 tablespoon olive oil
2 large Bosc pears, peeled, cored, and chopped
1 small shallot, peeled and minced
4 cups dandelion greens, chopped
salt and pepper
1 tablespoon balsamic vinegar

In a medium skillet, melt butter with olive oil. Add pears and cook until soft, about 2–3 minutes. Add shallots and cook 1 minute more. Stir in dandelion greens and cook 2 minutes more. Season lightly with salt and pepper, and sprinkle with vinegar.

Apple-Jalapeño Red Cabbage Salad

RÖDKÅLSALLAD MED ÄPPLEN SERVES 4–6

Cabbage salad is a common accompaniment to traditional Swedish dishes of winter, when the soil is frozen and greenhouses are closed for the season. The traditional recipe uses a quarter cup of red currant jelly, 1 teaspoon Dijon mustard, and lemon. The recipe here uses spicy apple-jalapeño jelly.

4 cups red cabbage (¼ head), shredded
2 green apples, peeled, cored, quartered, and sliced thin
1 tablespoon fresh flat-leaf parsley, minced
¼ cup apple-jalapeño jelly
zest and juice from 1 lemon (3 tablespoons)

In a medium-size bowl, combine all ingredients and marinate for a minimum of 1 hour before serving.

Variation

For hot salad: In a medium saucepan add all ingredients and cook over very low heat for 1 hour. Add water if necessary.

Pizza Salad

PIZZASALLAD SERVES 4

Swedish pizza is usually made with a multitude of gourmet toppings, such as mussels, arctic shrimp, mushrooms, pineapple, ham, and green peppers. This salad recipe is traditionally served with pizza.

Swedish pizza, along with cabbage salad, is always eaten with a fork and a knife.

2 cups green cabbage (¼ head), sliced very thin
2 green apples, peeled and shredded
½ small yellow onion, peeled and sliced thin
½ red bell pepper, seeded and sliced thin
½ teaspoon fennel seeds
¼ cup plain whole-milk yogurt
¼ cup lemon juice
⅛ cup white-wine vinegar
salt and pepper

Mix all ingredients and season to taste with salt and pepper. Marinate in the refrigerator for a minimum of 1 hour before serving.

Brussels Sprouts with Caramelized Onions and Italian Sausage

BRYSSELKÅL MED LÖK OCH KORV SERVES 4

When boiled or steamed, Brussels sprouts tend to develop a strong, bitter flavor. Here, the sprouts are sliced julienne and quickly sautéed with sausage and onion.

3 tablespoons olive oil, divided
1 small onion, peeled and sliced thin
3 cloves garlic, minced fine
1 hot Italian sausage, casing removed
8–10 Brussels sprouts, tough ends trimmed
1 tablespoon balsamic vinegar
salt and pepper

In a medium skillet, heat 1 tablespoon olive oil. Combine onion, garlic, and sausage and cook over low heat, breaking sausage into small pieces. Cook until onion begins to brown and sausage is completely cooked, about 5 minutes.

While onion and sausage are cooking, cut the trimmed Brussels sprouts in half. Lay cut sides down on a cutting board and cut into very thin slices. Stir Brussels sprouts into the sausage mixture; drizzle with remaining 2 tablespoons olive oil and cook while stirring, about 4 minutes. Add vinegar and season to taste with salt and pepper.

White Bean Salad with Roasted Red Peppers and Cherry Tomatoes

VITBÖNSSALLAD SERVES 6–8

This white bean salad can be eaten alone or served as a side dish to fish, chicken, or any meats.

2 ½ cups small white navy beans (1 pound)
2 quarts chicken broth
1 bay leaf
6 tablespoons olive oil, divided
1 tablespoon salt
1 red bell pepper, roasted, peeled, and minced
2 cups cherry tomatoes, halved
1 clove garlic, peeled and minced
2 tablespoons balsamic vinegar
2 tablespoons fresh basil, sliced julienne
salt and pepper to taste
1 bunch dandelion greens or arugula, minced

In a large stockpot cover beans with cold water and soak overnight. Drain water and discard any broken beans. Return beans to pot and add broth, bay leaf, and enough water (if needed) to cover beans by 2 inches. Simmer over low heat according to package directions or until beans are just done, about 1 ½ hours. Remove from heat and stir in 2 tablespoons olive oil and 1 tablespoon salt. Let steep for 30 minutes.

While beans are cooking, in a small bowl combine roasted red pepper, tomatoes, 4 tablespoons olive oil, garlic, balsamic vinegar, and basil. Marinate for a minimum of 30 minutes at room temperature. Drain and discard the liquid from the beans and transfer them to a serving bowl. Add red-pepper mixture, and season with additional salt and pepper to taste. Stir in dandelion greens. Serve at room temperature.

Refried Hot and Sweet Swedish Brown Beans

BRUNA BÖNOR SERVES 4

Swedish baked brown beans are traditionally eaten with pork (page 46) on Shrove Tuesday. For the traditional recipe, cook an 18-ounce package of Swedish brown beans according to package directions or until just done, about 1 ½ to 2 hours. Season with ¼ cup vinegar and ¼ cup maple syrup. Salt and pepper to taste. Chilies and bacon are added to this recipe and the beans are refried, creating a sweet, spicy, and delicious dish.

½ package Swedish brown beans (9 ounces), or substitute
    other brown beans such as pinto or small red beans
6 strips bacon, preferably apple-wood smoked, cut crosswise into ½-inch pieces
½ onion, peeled and chopped fine
½ jalapeño pepper, seeded and minced
¼ cup maple syrup
¼ cup balsamic vinegar
3 tablespoons vegetable oil
salt and pepper to taste

Cover beans with 2 inches of water and soak overnight. Drain beans and cover with fresh water and cook according to package directions or until beans are just done, about 1 ½ hours. Drain beans, reserving bean broth.

While beans are cooking, in a medium skillet fry bacon until browned and crisp, about 5 minutes. Drain on paper towels. Reserve 2 tablespoons of bacon fat in the pan. Cook onion and jalapeño in the fat until onion is translucent, about 5 minutes. Transfer cooked beans, bacon, onion-jalapeño mixture, and 1 cup of bean broth to a food processor. Pulse for a few seconds until half the mixture is puréed but half remains whole. Transfer to a large bowl and stir syrup and vinegar into bean mixture. Add additional bean broth if the mixture is too thick. In a large skillet heat the vegetable oil, add beans, and cook while stirring, about 5–8 minutes. Season with salt and pepper to taste.

Red Beet Latkes with Crème Fraîche and Chives

RÖDBETSBIFFAR **MAKES 20 TINY LATKES OR 4 MEDIUM SIZE**

Traditionally, red beet latkes would be served almost like veggie burgers, with boiled potatoes (of course) and a side dish of vegetables. I love preparing tiny red beet latkes as an appetizer garnished with a heaping teaspoon of crème fraîche.

Ground beef mixed with shredded cooked beets and raw onion and formed into hamburger patties is a Swedish favorite called *biff à la Lindström*.

1 medium beet (1 cup), boiled or roasted, peeled, and grated
1 medium russet potato (1 cup), boiled, peeled, and grated
½ small yellow onion (¼ cup), peeled and grated
1 tablespoon dry bread crumbs
½ egg, lightly beaten
1 teaspoon fresh lemon juice
1 tablespoon fresh flat-leaf parsley, minced
salt and pepper to taste
2 tablespoons butter
1 tablespoon olive oil
½ cup sour cream
1 tablespoon fresh chives, minced

In a medium bowl, combine cooked beets and potatoes with onion, bread crumbs, egg, lemon juice, and parsley. Season with salt and pepper to taste. In a large skillet, melt butter with olive oil. Form small patties/latkes with potato-beet mixture and fry on each side until golden brown, about 2–3 minutes per side. Garnish with sour cream and chives.

Lentil Salad with Radishes

LINSSALLAD **SERVES 4**

This salad is great with grilled salmon (page 64–65) or roasted chicken (page 56). Make sure not to over-cook the lentils as the salad is best when they are slightly crunchy.

1 cup brown lentils
2 ½ cups chicken or vegetable broth
1 bay leaf
2 strips bacon, sliced julienne and cooked until crisp
½ cup radishes, sliced thin
½ cup fresh parsley, chopped coarse
3 shallots (¼ cup), peeled and minced

Dressing:
1 garlic clove, minced
1 teaspoon Dijon mustard
1 tablespoon fresh lemon juice
2 teaspoons balsamic vinegar
salt and pepper to taste
2 tablespoons olive oil

In a medium saucepan, combine lentils, broth, bay leaf, and enough water to cover the lentils by 2 inches. Bring to a boil, reduce heat, and let simmer until just done but still slightly crunchy, about 15–20 minutes. Drain and transfer to a medium-size bowl. Set aside.

To prepare the dressing, combine garlic, mustard, lemon juice, and vinegar in a small bowl. Season with salt and pepper. Slowly whisk in olive oil until combined and pour dressing over lentils.

Add bacon, radishes, parsley, and shallots to lentils. Serve cold or at room temperature.

NOTES

NOTES

Sandwiches

Swedish sandwiches are scrumptious, delicate works of art eaten with a knife and a fork. They are beautifully decorated, and the crown jewel of all Swedish sandwiches is the *smörgåstårta* (sandwich cake).

Sandwich cake is reserved for the most special of occasions. Like a wedding cake, it is rich and to be admired as much as it is to be eaten. But unlike a wedding cake, sandwich cake is the main course, not the sweet ending. It can be made with numerous ingredients and garnishes: layered with soft white and brown breads, spread with seafood or meats, and garnished with smoked salmon, caviar, tiny arctic shrimp, and cucumber rosettes. I prefer taking the components of sandwich cake and creating little tea sandwiches that are delicious and artful but not so filling.

Swedish sandwiches in general never have more than two to three thin layers of cheeses or meats, and never resemble impossible-to-eat Subway-style sandwiches. In our home in the evenings, we would often make hot sandwiches with ham, shrimp béchamel sauce, and melted Gruyère cheese. And for that special Saturday night when *Dynasty* (or any American show) was broadcast, a *löjrom* (whitefish roe) sandwich would be our treat. Sitting in front of the television eating whitefish roe sandwiches with my grandmother and mother seemed more special than any fabulous Hollywood party I go to today.

Whether you are making an elaborate sandwich cake, a simple sandwich for lunch, or a hot sandwich for a late night snack, it is important that you make the sandwich look beautiful. Use only the best ingredients, and serve it on your nice china with your silver tableware.

PLT: Pancetta, Lettuce, and Tomato Sandwich
SKINKSMÖRGÅS SERVES 4

My favorite evening sandwich when I was a young girl was soft white bread spread with sweet butter, stacked with a slice of ham or pancetta and a slice of vine-ripened tomato, covered with creamy béchamel sauce with wild mushrooms, then topped with a slice of Gruyère cheese. The sandwich was baked in the oven until hot and bubbly (page 102). It was heaven, especially when enjoyed with Swedish channel 1 or 2, the only television stations we could tune in to at the time.

This recipe for a PLT sandwich holds the béchamel, but not the essential flavor.

4 slices of pancetta (1/8 inch thick) or 8 slices bacon
4 tablespoons mayonnaise
1 teaspoon garlic, minced
1 tablespoon fresh lemon juice
8 slices white country bread
olive oil spray
3 large, ripe heirloom tomatoes
2 tablespoons olive oil
2 tablespoons balsamic vinegar
salt and pepper to taste
2 cups lettuce leaves, dandelion greens, arugula, or other bittersweet lettuce

Preheat oven to 400 degrees Fahrenheit. Arrange pancetta or bacon on a rimmed baking sheet. Bake according to package directions or until crisp, about 15 minutes. Drain on paper towels.

While pancetta is baking, in a small bowl combine mayonnaise, garlic, and lemon juice.

Preheat an outdoor grill or stovetop grill pan. Spray bread with olive oil spray on both sides. Grill for a few minutes on each side until grill marks appear. Cut tomatoes into thin slices, sprinkle with olive oil and vinegar, and season with salt and pepper. Divide and spread mayonnaise mixture on the bread. Divide tomatoes and lettuce on bread slices and top each sandwich with 1 slice of pancetta (or 2 slices of bacon). Top with second slice of bread.

SLT: Salmon, Lettuce, and Tomato Sandwich

LAXSMÖRGÅS **SERVES 4**

A Swedish take on the classic BLT sandwich. You may also add avocado, which goes very well with salmon.

4 tablespoons mayonnaise
1 teaspoon garlic, minced
1 tablespoon fresh lemon juice
8 slices whole-wheat bread
olive oil spray
3 large, ripe heirloom tomatoes
2 tablespoons olive oil
2 tablespoons balsamic vinegar
salt and pepper to taste
2 cups lettuce leaves, dandelion greens, arugula, or other bittersweet lettuce
8 slices of gravlax (page 61) or smoked salmon

Preheat outdoor grill or stovetop grill pan. In a small bowl combine mayonnaise, garlic, and lemon juice. Spray bread with olive oil on both sides. Grill for a few minutes on each side until grill marks appear. Cut tomatoes into thin slices, sprinkle with olive oil and vinegar, and season with salt and pepper to taste. Divide and spread mayonnaise mixture on bread. Divide tomatoes and lettuce on bread slices, and top each sandwich with two slices of gravlax. Top with the second slice of bread.

Grilled Cheese Panini

GRILLAD OSTSMÖRGÅS SERVES 4

Every Swede loves melted cheese, and I am no exception. Most of the sandwiches we ate when I was growing up included melted cheese and béchamel sauce. Just the thought of it transports me to a time and a place when my grandmother was alive and she was the queen of our tiny home. When I would cut my hot, buttery, aromatic sandwich into tiny pieces with a knife and a fork, my home was a castle and I was its princess, albeit with pimples and an Afro. But I did not need a prince to rescue me. I had a great sandwich on my plate.

If you would like to serve this cheese sandwich with béchamel sauce, melt 2 tablespoons of butter in a heavy saucepan over low heat, whisk in 1 ½ tablespoons of flour, and incorporate well into butter. Whisk in ¾ cup whole milk, stirring constantly, and simmer until sauce begins to thicken, about 5 minutes. Season with salt and pepper to taste. On a slice of buttered white bread topped with 1 slice of ham and 1 thin slice of tomato, spread 2 tablespoons of béchamel sauce and add 1 slice of Gruyère cheese. Bake until cheese begins to brown and bubble. (Or stir ½ cup of arctic shrimp into béchamel sauce with 1 table-spoon of finely chopped dill, or ½ cup cooked wild mushrooms with 1 tablespoon of finely chopped parsley, and assemble as described above.)

8 slices country white bread
3 tablespoons butter
8 slices Gruyère cheese
olive oil spray
8 slices Swiss cheese

Preheat a panini press, stovetop grill pan, or outdoor grill. Spread one side of each slice of bread with butter. Divide cheese on half of the slices and top with remaining slices. Spray top slice with olive oil and place sprayed side down on the press or grill. Spray other side of bread with olive oil and cook until grill marks appear on the first side. Flip and grill the other side until cheese melts and both sides are browned.

Sandwich Cake (Traditional)

SMÖRGÅSTÅRTA SERVES 16–20

At least once a year back home there would be reason to serve sandwich cake: a graduation, a christening, or a birthday. It is usually served in midafternoon, not for lunch or dinner.

A small slice of this rich, filling treat goes a long way. For a taste of traditional Sweden, make your own showstopping sandwich cake with this mayonnaise/seafood-based recipe.

1 loaf unsliced white bread, preferably pain de mie
1 loaf unsliced brown bread
assorted fillings, at least three, each about 1 ½ to 2 cups:
  cream cheese, mixed with sweet butter and fresh herbs (page 109)
  liver paste
  egg salad (page 106)
  hard-boiled eggs, chopped fine and mixed with mayonnaise, whitefish roe, and dill
  cottage cheese mixed with drained crushed pineapple
  cooked arctic shrimp, chopped fine, with mayonnaise, cucumber, and dill
  chicken salad (page 110)
  salmon tartar (page 63)
  cooked salmon mixed with crème fraîche, mayonnaise, prepared horseradish, lemon juice, and fresh dill

Remove bread crusts and slice each loaf horizontally into 4–6 slices. On a serving platter, lay 2 slices of white bread side by side. Spread a thin layer (about 1 ½ cups to 2 cups) of one topping evenly over the bread. Top with 2 lengthwise slices of brown bread and spread a thin layer (about 1 ½ cups to 2 cups) of another topping. Use at least three different fillings and continue until all layers of the bread have been used. Cover sandwiches tightly with plastic food wrap, lay a small, lightweight cutting board on top, and refrigerate for a minimum of 4 hours. After the sandwiches have chilled they can be covered with any of the toppings below:

cream cheese mixed with sweet butter
mayonnaise or sour cream
gravlax or smoked salmon, sliced thin
cooked arctic shrimp
hard-boiled eggs, sliced thin
cucumber, sliced thin
radishes, sliced thin
Gruyère or other cheese, sliced and rolled into rosettes
ham, turkey, or other sandwich meats, sliced and rolled into rosettes
small canned mussels, drained
red or black caviar
tomato wedges, sliced

lemon, sliced thin
fresh herbs such as dill or parsley, chopped fine

Spread a thick layer of mayonnaise, sour cream, or cream cheese evenly over the top and sides of sandwich cake. Cover sides with herbs and other toppings. Create your masterpiece by decoratively arranging assorted toppings on the cake—perhaps a row of gravlax rosettes, followed by a row of minced hard-boiled egg, a row of caviar, and a row of cucumber. Any combination can be used.

To serve, cut into $\frac{1}{2}$-inch slices and serve on a small plate with a dessert fork.

Sandwich Cake (Grilled Vegetable)

SMÖRGÅSTÅRTA MED GRILLADE GRÖNSAKER SERVES 16–20

In this variation of sandwich cake, grilled vegetables and goat cheese have replaced the mayonnaise and seafood. Feel free to use any combination of vegetables and meats that you like. Salami, ham, olives, and artichoke hearts all would work great.

1 loaf unsliced white bread, preferably pain de mie
1 loaf unsliced brown bread
2 eggplants, sliced thin lengthwise
6 large green zucchini, sliced thin lengthwise
olive oil spray
salt and pepper to taste
2 garlic cloves, peeled and minced
1 tablespoon balsamic vinegar
2 goat cheese logs (4 ounces each)
2 15-ounce containers whipped cream cheese
5 large red peppers, roasted and peeled
1 bunch baby arugula
12 ounces prosciutto, sliced thin
24 ounces tiny mozzarella balls (boccini)

Preheat an outdoor grill or stovetop grill pan. Remove crusts and slice each loaf horizontally into 4–6 slices. On a serving platter, lay 2 slices of the white bread side by side. Spray eggplant and zucchini with olive oil and grill on both sides until grill marks appear and vegetables are cooked. Season vegetables with salt, pepper, and garlic, and sprinkle with vinegar.

In a mixing bowl, combine goat cheese and cream cheese. On the bottom layer of the bread spread a thin layer of cheese mixture. Evenly cover with eggplant. Top with the second layer of bread and spread with a thin layer of cheese mixture and grilled zucchini. Add the third layer of bread and spread with cheese mixture, roasted red peppers, and arugula.

Using other fillings of your choice, continue until all layers of bread have been used. Cover sandwiches tightly with plastic food wrap, lay a small, lightweight cutting board on top, and refrigerate for a minimum of 4 hours. After sandwich has chilled, spread top and sides with the remaining cheese mixture. Garnish the sides with prosciutto and the top with mozzarella balls.

Curried Egg Salad Sandwiches
with Sunflower Sprouts

SMÖRGÅS MED ÄGGSALLAD **SERVES 6**

The Swedish sandwich is a small objet d'art, so take your time to decoratively layer the ingredients and garnishes. This filling can also be used for *smörgåstårta* (page 103).

6 hard-boiled eggs, chopped
1 teaspoon curry powder
4 tablespoons mayonnaise
salt and pepper to taste
6 slices whole-wheat bread
1 cup sunflower sprouts
4 radishes, sliced very thin

In a small bowl combine eggs, curry powder, and mayonnaise. Season with salt and pepper to taste. Evenly divide egg mixture over bread, and garnish with sunflower sprouts and radishes.

To serve as a sandwich, serve one open-faced sandwich per person. To serve as an appetizer, remove the crusts and cut each slice of bread twice diagonally to create four small triangles per slice of bread.

Arctic Shrimp and Cucumber Sandwiches with Chipotle Crème

RÄKSMÖRGÅS SERVES 4

Once in a while my childhood friends and I would ride our bikes into the center of town to go shopping. After shopping we would stop for a midday snack at a store restaurant, that served exquisite shrimp sandwiches. We would choose from rows of small sandwiches displayed behind a little glass window, lifting the window to make our selection and put it on our tray. Served on fine china, the sandwich was cut into bite-size pieces with a knife and fork.

Here, the classic sandwich is spiced up using the adobo sauce from canned chipotle peppers. To make the original sandwich, replace the adobo sauce with 1 tablespoon lemon juice.

8 tablespoons mayonnaise
1 teaspoon adobo sauce from canned chipotle peppers
4 slices white bread
4 leaves butter lettuce
4 hard-boiled eggs, sliced thin
1 pound arctic shrimp (2 cups), cooked
½ cucumber, preferably European seedless, sliced thin
1 whole lemon with peel, sliced thin
dill sprigs for garnish

In a small bowl, combine mayonnaise and adobo sauce. Spread half the mayonnaise on bread slices and top with lettuce and hard-boiled eggs. Spoon remaining mayonnaise over eggs and evenly divide the shrimp. Garnish with cucumber, lemon, and dill.

To serve as a sandwich, serve one open-faced sandwich per person. To serve as an appetizer, remove the crust and cut each slice of bread twice diagonally to create four triangles per slice of bread.

Gravlax and Nasturtium Sandwiches with Mustard-Dill Sauce

GRAVLAXSMÖRGÅS MED SENAPSSÅS SERVES 4

Gravlax is one of the most popular ways to eat salmon in Sweden. It is eaten for breakfast, lunch, and dinner, and it is almost always served during parties and special events. Layer the salmon decoratively over the bread and garnish with dill or nasturtium flowers.

1 tablespoon butter
4 slices white bread
4 leaves butter lettuce
12 thin slices gravlax (page 61)
4 tablespoons mustard-dill sauce (page 62)
½ cucumber, preferably European seedless, sliced thin
fresh dill sprigs for garnish
4 nasturtium flowers (optional)

Spread a thin coat of butter on each slice of bread and top with lettuce. Decoratively place 3 slices of gravlax per sandwich on top of the lettuce. Drizzle 1 tablespoon of mustard-dill sauce over the gravlax. Garnish with cucumber slices, dill, and nasturtium flowers, if desired.

To serve as a sandwich, serve one open-faced sandwich per person. To serve as an appetizer, remove the crust and cut each slice of bread twice diagonally to create four small triangles per slice of bread.

Smoked Salmon Sandwiches with Herb Butter

GRAVLAXSMÖRGÅS MED ÖRTSMÖR SERVES 4

These make great tea sandwiches. The filling can also be used in *smörgåstårta* (page 103).

4 tablespoons butter
2 tablespoons cream cheese
½ cup assorted fresh herbs, such as dill, parsley, or chervil
zest of 1 lemon
4 slices white bread
12 slices smoked salmon or gravlax (page 61)
½ cucumber, preferably European seedless, sliced thin
fresh dill sprigs

In a food processor or in a bowl, combine butter, cream cheese, herbs, and lemon zest until well combined. On each slice of bread, spread an even layer of the herb butter. Decoratively divide smoked salmon over bread, and garnish with cucumbers and dill.

To serve as a sandwich, serve one open-faced sandwich per person. To serve as tea sandwiches, remove the crust and cut each slice twice diagonally to create four small triangles per slice of bread.

Lime-Marinated Chicken Salad Sandwiches with Radicchio and Olives
SMÖRGÅS MED KYCKLINGSALLAD SERVES 4

This zesty chicken salad with lime juice, olives, and radicchio makes great sandwiches and appetizers. For an appetizer, place a small dollop of the salad on a mini potato latke (page 32) or on a piece of bread cut into small rounds with a cookie cutter.

2 half chicken breasts (about 2 pounds), bone in and skin on
salt and pepper to taste
¼ cup fresh lime juice
2 tablespoons fresh lemon juice
¼ teaspoon sugar
½ teaspoon paprika
¼ teaspoon cayenne pepper
2 shallots (3 tablespoons), peeled and chopped fine
3 tablespoons mayonnaise
½ cup fresh flat-leaf parsley, chopped
½ cup radicchio, chopped
½ cup pitted kalamata olives, chopped
8 slices bread, preferably olive bread

Place chicken breasts in a medium saucepan and cover with cold water. Bring to a gentle boil for 5 minutes. Cover, turn off heat, and steep until done or juices run clear, about 30 minutes. If juices are still red, return chicken to pan and continue steeping until done. Remove from pan and let cool.

When cool, remove and discard bones and skin and chop the breast meat into fine pieces. Transfer chopped chicken to a bowl and season with salt and pepper, add lime and lemon juices, stir in all the other ingredients except the bread. Season with additional salt and pepper to taste.

Spread on the bread, either as an open-faced sandwich (garnished with parsley leaf) or topped with a second slice of bread.

Whitefish Roe Sandwiches with Chives and Shallots

SMÖRGÅS MED LÖJROM SERVES 4

In the dark, cold winter, my uncle would brave the negative 30 degrees Celsius temperature and head out alone with his fishing pole. He would go ice fishing in hopes of catching bleak, the native Scandinavian white-fleshed fish, also known as ocean gold.

Most times he would return empty-handed, but we would always eagerly await his arrival, hoping for the treasured and hard-to-obtain roe. I do not remember eating the whitefish itself, but the roe was a delicious and magical treat. The tiny, bright golden roe nuggets are slippery and crunchy.

We used whitefish roe mostly as a topping for gourmet sandwiches, but it also makes an excellent sauce, folded into crème fraîche with a sprinkling of dill, and served with salmon or arctic char (page 68).

The combination of toasted country bread with sweet melted butter and salty roe makes these sandwiches divine.

Bleak roe (*löjrom*) is not available in the United States. Substitute whitefish roe or Lake Superior herring roe.

4 slices white bread
2 tablespoons butter
8 ounces whitefish or Lake Superior herring roe
1 shallot, peeled and chopped fine
1 teaspoon coarse ground black pepper
4 fresh chive sprigs, chopped fine

In a toaster, toast bread until golden then generously spread with butter. Divide roe evenly on the 4 slices of bread. Sprinkle with shallots and black pepper. Garnish with chive. Serve while bread is hot and roe is cool.

Variation SERVES 4

To serve as appetizer: Remove the crust and cut each piece twice diagonally to create four small triangles from each slice of bread. Garnish with chives. Serve at once.

NOTES

NOTES

Eggs, Waffles, and Pancakes

    While my cousins and I were out fishing with my uncle at the lake by our summerhouse, my aunt would prepare us breakfast. When we returned to the house, we were greeted with the fragrance of bacon and a lofty golden pancake (page 116) baking in the oven like a billowy cloud of goodness. My aunt would fill this light and luscious pancake with crispy bacon and serve it with lingonberries and a dusting of powdered sugar. Other times she would make stacks of silver-dollar-size Swedish pancakes (page 118) for me and my cousins. We would top the towers of golden pancakes with freshly picked ruby-red currants, strawberries, or raspberries that spilled over and down the sides. We would finish them off with drizzled syrup, a dusting of powdered sugar to make them look like snow-covered mountain peaks, and a small dollop of crème fraîche.

  When our little boat pulled up to shore, we kids would scramble off toward the heavenly scents coming from the cottage, and leave my uncle to clean and put away the catch. At the table, my aunt would hand each of us an assembled plate of pancakes and tell us that the person who found the hidden golden berry in his or her stack would not have to help with cleanup that day. Like the mattresses in the story of the princess and the pea, the pancakes were stacked high, and as much as we searched for the hidden berry, we never found it. Maybe we were too hungry or the pancakes were too delicious for us to search thoroughly. Maybe she never hid a berry in the stack, knowing she needed us all for various tasks that day. I will never know, but I can say that we all felt like royalty sitting in the tiny cottage by the edge of the lake, with our regal towers of stacked Swedish pancakes.

  Our plates were always scraped clean, which was a good thing. Because our summerhouse did not have running water, we had to take the dishes outside to wash them in a bucket of lake water by the forest's edge. It was a small inconvenience for such a memorable meal.

Oven-Baked Swedish Bacon Pancake, 4-1-1 Pancake

FLÄSKPANNKAKA SERVES 4

These pillowy, golden mounds filled with bacon are an original that simply cannot be improved. The recipe is easy to remember: 4 eggs, 1 cup flour, and 1 cup milk (4-1-1).

6 ounces salted pork fat or bacon (optional)
4 large eggs
1 cup milk
1 cup all-purpose flour
zest of 1 lemon
¼ cup butter
powdered sugar
lingonberry preserve or other berries
whipped cream, sweetened with sugar and beaten until soft peaks form

Preheat oven to 450 degrees Fahrenheit. To remove excess saltiness of pork fat, cover it in water in a small saucepan and cook for 2 minutes. Drain water and repeat process. Cut pork fat into small cubes. In a large skillet cook over medium-high heat until crisp. Drain on paper towels.

In the bowl of a food processor, combine eggs, milk, flour, and lemon zest. Process until blended (or whisk together in a large bowl). Place a 3-quart paella pan (or other low-rimmed baking dish) in the oven with the butter until butter is melted. Remove and tilt the pan so butter evenly coats the bottom. Pour pancake mixture into the hot pan and evenly sprinkle pork over the batter. Return pan to oven and bake pancake until golden and puffy, about 20 minutes. Serve at once. Dust with powdered sugar and serve with berries and whipped cream.

Waffles with Lingonberries

VÅFFLOR SERVES 4–6

This classic Swedish recipe of light, crispy waffles is perfection. Swedish waffles are traditionally cooked in a cast iron skillet that makes one waffle with five heart shapes. You may prepare them in any waffle iron, but a Belgian waffle iron is not recommended because Swedish waffles are usually made very thin.

2 cups all-purpose flour
1 ¼ cups water
2 cups heavy whipping cream, divided
3 tablespoons sugar
2 teaspoons vanilla extract
3 ½ teaspoons baking powder
zest of 1 lemon (optional)
whipped cream, lingonberry preserve, and syrup (to garnish)

In a medium-size bowl, whisk flour, water, and ¼ cup whipping cream. Add sugar, vanilla, baking powder, and lemon zest (if desired) and beat until smooth.

Preheat waffle iron. In a separate bowl, beat remaining cream until it holds stiff peaks and gently fold it into the batter. When iron is hot, spoon ⅓ cup batter (depending on size of iron) onto its surface. Cook until waffle is brown and crisp, about 4 minutes. Repeat with remaining batter. Serve with whipped cream, lingonberry preserve (page 178), or other berries and syrup.

Swedish Pancakes

PANNKAKOR SERVES 4

Swedish pancakes are one of Sweden's best-known food exports. Served with sprinkled sugar, lingonberry preserve (page 178), and sour cream, they are traditionally eaten as a dessert on Thursdays with yellow pea soup (page 7).

Swedish pancakes are essentially a crêpe, eaten sweet for breakfast or dessert or savory for supper with assorted fillings. They may be made the size of a crêpe or a silver dollar.

3 eggs
1 cup all-purpose flour
1 tablespoon sugar
1 ½ cups milk
3 tablespoons butter, melted

additional butter (to cook crêpes)
sugar, lingonberry preserve, and sour cream (to garnish)

Blend all ingredients in a food processor until combined. Heat a 7-inch nonstick or cast iron skillet until hot. Add a small amount of butter and immediately pour in one ladle full of batter; quickly tilt pan to spread batter evenly over the bottom. When pancake edges are dry and bubbles begin to appear in the center, flip it with a spatula and cook the other side until lightly brown. Repeat with the remaining batter, stacking the pancakes on a plate. Serve sprinkled with sugar, lingonberry preserve, and sour cream as dessert or breakfast, or use fillings (pages 119–21) and eat as a light supper.

Swedish Pancakes with Bacon, Shrimp, and Corn Filling

PANNKAKOR MED BACON, RÄKOR, OCH MAJSFYLLNING SERVES 4

Swedish pancakes are often served savory for a light supper or a snack. You may substitute cooked crayfish for shrimp in this recipe if you have leftovers from a crayfish feast (page 78).

5 slices bacon, cut into medium pieces
½ pound raw shrimp (2 cups), chopped
2 tablespoons butter, divided
salt and pepper to taste
1 cup corn, fresh or frozen
juice of 1 lemon (3 tablespoons)
¼ cup fresh flat-leaf parsley, chopped
4 Swedish pancakes/crêpes (page 118)

In a skillet over high heat, cook bacon until crisp. Drain on paper towels. In a small sauté pan, cook shrimp in 1 tablespoon butter until pink, about 2 minutes. Salt and pepper to taste and add corn and lemon juice. When juice reaches a low boil, whisk in remaining tablespoon of butter until melted. Sprinkle with bacon and parsley. Place crêpes on a plate. Divide filling equally among the crêpes and roll up. Serve at once.

Swedish Pancakes with Wild-Mushroom Filling

PANNKAKOR MED SVAMPFYLLNING SERVES 4

These Swedish pancakes are filled with mushrooms and slightly reduced cream. If you prefer a thicker sauce, prepare a béchamel sauce (page 102) and add the cooked mushrooms and parsley.

1 tablespoon butter
1 tablespoon olive oil
¼ cup onion, chopped fine
2 cups assorted wild mushrooms, brushed clean and chopped
salt and pepper to taste
2 tablespoons fresh lemon juice
1 cup heavy cream
4 Swedish pancakes/crêpes (page 118)
4 sprigs parsley, chopped

In a medium sauté pan, melt butter with olive oil over medium heat and cook onion until translucent, about 2–3 minutes. Add mushrooms and cook 5 minutes more. Season with salt and pepper to taste. Add lemon juice and cream. Let cook until cream begins to thicken, about 5 minutes more. Place crêpes on a plate. Sprinkle with parsley. Divide the filling equally among crêpes and roll up. Serve at once.

Swedish Pancakes with Arctic Shrimp Filling

PANNKAKOR MED RÄKFYLLNING SERVES 4

Fresh dill and tiny arctic shrimp make up the filling in this recipe. You may substitute cooked crayfish for shrimp in this recipe if you have leftovers from a crayfish feast (page 78). If you prefer a thicker sauce, prepare a béchamel sauce (page 102) and add cooked shrimp, dill, and lime juice.

½ cup white wine
1 tablespoon fresh lemon juice
1 cup heavy cream
½ pound arctic shrimp (1 cup), cooked
1 tablespoon fresh dill, chopped
salt and pepper to taste
4 Swedish pancakes/crêpes (page 118)

In a medium sauté pan, combine wine and lemon juice and simmer until reduced to a few tablespoons, about 10 minutes. Add cream and cook until sauce begins to thicken, about 5 minutes more. Add shrimp and dill and season with salt and pepper to taste. Divide filling equally among the crêpes and roll up. Serve at once.

Lost Eggs with Serrano Ham and Baby Spinach

FÖRLORADE ÄGG MED SKINKA SERVES 4–6

This breakfast dish can be assembled the night before and baked just before serving. Served with toasted country bread and fresh squeezed orange juice, it makes a perfect Sunday morning treat.

1 tablespoon butter
6 thin slices serrano ham, or cooked pancetta or bacon
1 cup baby spinach
1 tomato, peeled, cored, and chopped fine
6 large eggs
salt and pepper
½ cup Parmesan cheese, grated

Preheat oven to 400 degrees Fahrenheit. Butter a small baking dish or six individual ramekins. Arrange ham on the bottom and top with spinach and tomato. Carefully crack eggs so they nest into pockets of spinach. Season lightly with salt and pepper. Sprinkle Parmesan on top. Bake until eggs are just cooked and cheese is melted, about 8 minutes.

Fresh Herb Omelet with Gravlax

GRAVLAXOMELETT MED ÖRTER SERVES 4

The French bistro in Luleå where I worked was open on Sundays for breakfast only. Fresh orange juice and an herb omelet with gravlax were the must-order brunch items. A machine in the dining room cut and juiced fresh oranges to order. We served the juice in frosty glasses chilled in the freezer, which instantly turned the room-temperature beverage ice cold—a novelty in our tiny town.

8 eggs, lightly beaten
½ cup assorted fresh herbs, such as dill, parsley, chives, chervil, and basil
salt and pepper
2 tablespoons butter
4 ounces goat cheese, crumbled
8 slices gravlax (page 61) or smoked salmon
¼ cup red onion, minced fine

In a small bowl, mix eggs and herbs. Season lightly with salt and pepper. In a small, nonstick skillet, melt a fourth of the butter. Add a small ladle full of the egg/herb mixture. Stir a few times with a spatula and cook until eggs begin to set. Add a fourth of the cheese, 2 slices of gravlax, and a fourth of the onion. Fold omelet in half and transfer to a plate. Continue with remaining egg/herb mixture, making 4 individual omelets.

Lox and Cream Cheese Quiche

LAX OCH OSTPAJ SERVES 4–6

Hold the bagels! This quiche with lox and cream cheese makes a terrific treat for Sunday brunch.

Crust:
1 ¼ cups all-purpose flour
1 teaspoon salt
1 teaspoon dry mustard
1 teaspoon ground paprika
½ cup butter (8 tablespoons), cut into small cubes
1 egg yolk
1–3 tablespoons ice water

In a food processor combine flour, salt, mustard, and paprika. Pulse once, add butter, and pulse a few more times until mixture resembles coarse meal. Add egg yolk and water and pulse one more time or until the dough just comes together. Transfer dough to a floured surface and knead for 1 minute. Cover in plastic food wrap and chill in the refrigerator 1 hour.

Preheat oven to 350 degrees Fahrenheit. On a floured surface, roll out dough, turning twice, until it is large enough to fill a 9-inch pie pan. Transfer dough to pie pan; trim any overhang. Bake crust for 15 minutes. Let cool before adding filling.

Filling:
6 eggs
1 cup heavy cream
1 cup milk
salt and pepper
1 cup gravlax (page 61) or smoked salmon, chopped
2 Roma tomatoes, cored, seeded, and chopped
½ cup cream cheese, cut into chunks
¼ cup red onion, minced
2 tablespoons fresh dill, chopped
2 tablespoons Parmesan cheese, grated

Preheat oven to 375 degrees Fahrenheit. In a medium bowl, whisk eggs, cream, and milk. Season lightly with salt and pepper. Stir in gravlax, tomatoes, cream cheese, onion, and dill. Pour into pre-baked pie shell and sprinkle with Parmesan. Bake until just set, about 45 minutes. Let rest a few minutes before slicing.

Potato Quiche with Prosciutto

POTATISPAJ MED FLÄSK SERVES 4–6

Creamy potatoes, salty prosciutto, and bittersweet dandelion greens make up the filling of this quiche. Serve for lunch with a green salad.

Prebaked crust (page 124)

Filling:
1 tablespoon butter
1 tablespoon olive oil
¾ cup russet potato (1 medium), peeled and cut into small cubes
6 eggs
1 cup heavy cream
1 cup milk
salt and pepper to taste
1 cup prosciutto, cooked bacon, or other ham, chopped
2 Roma tomatoes, cored, seeded, and diced medium
½ cup dandelion greens, spinach, or arugula, chopped medium
½ cup Gruyère cheese, grated
2 tablespoons Parmesan cheese, grated

Preheat oven to 375 degrees Fahrenheit. In a small pan, heat butter and oil. Add potato and cook until lightly browned and cooked through, about 5–8 minutes. Season with salt and pepper to taste. In a medium bowl, whisk eggs, cream, and milk. Season lightly with salt and pepper. Stir in potatoes, prosciutto, tomatoes, greens, and Gruyère. Pour into prebaked pie shell and sprinkle with Parmesan. Bake until just set, about 45 minutes. Let rest a few minutes before slicing.

Frittata with Potatoes, Salmon, and Tomatoes

POTATIS OCH LAXÄGGRÖRA SERVES 4

When you crave an egg breakfast but do not feel like flipping an omelet or making a crust for a quiche, a frittata is the perfect quick and easy alternative.

2 tablespoons olive oil
1 cup russet potato (1 medium), peeled and cut into small cubes
1 small onion, peeled and chopped
1 green bell pepper, chopped
salt and pepper
2 Roma tomatoes, peeled, seeded, and chopped
1 cup gravlax (page 61) or smoked salmon (4 ounces), diced
½ cup fresh flat-leaf parsley, chopped
6 eggs, lightly beaten
cucumber salsa (page 65) and sour cream (to garnish) (optional)

In a large cast iron skillet, heat olive oil over medium heat. Add potato, onion, and green pepper and cook until potato begins to soften and onion is translucent, about 5–8 minutes. Season lightly with salt and pepper. Add tomatoes, gravlax, and parsley. Pour eggs evenly over the top and cook until set, about 5–8 minutes. Flip frittata to brown the top for a few minutes, or place it under the broiler for a few minutes. If desired, serve with cucumber salsa and sour cream.

NOTES

Desserts, Pastries, and Bread

It seems I spent my entire childhood and adolescence trying to fit into a place I was not sure I belonged. Not being a classic blue-eyed blond, I never thought I would have the chance to be Santa Lucia at my school. But one Christmas, against all odds, I was voted Lucia. The Swedes, always looking to buck tradition, saw the exotic possibilities in a black Lucia. For the first time, I, the ugly duckling, straightened my back and lifted my head high as I wore the crown of lit candles, the white embroidered gown, and the shiny red belt. As I carried the tray of pastries, glimmering like treasures in the candlelight, a sense of dreams and hopes filled the room. For one rare and magical moment, I felt truly Swedish.

Growing up in the north of Sweden, I never saw another black person. Although my father was African American, I had not seen him since I was four years old. I would frequently scan LP covers of Diana Ross and Michael Jackson and imagine what it would be like to see someone like me. Then one summer when I was fourteen, my father invited me to America, and soon I was headed to a place where I thought I would fit right in.

I arrived for my two-week visit and saw other black people, of course—but for the first time in my life I felt like a foreigner. Maybe from the outside I blended in, but as I ate supersized Subway sandwiches overflowing with meats and salad, wrapped in messy paper with no silverware in sight, I felt utterly out of place.

When I returned to Luleå and climbed the stairs to my grandmother's apartment, the scent of cinnamon- and cardamom-laced bullar—a whole spread of freshly made fika—wafted down toward me to welcome me home. I knew then that even though I looked nothing like my friends and family, when I sat at the table for fika, I was (and always would be) Swedish.

Most recipes in this section have not been altered. They are sublimely delicious just the way they are.

Saffron and Raisin Buns (Santa Lucia Buns)

LUSSEKATTER **MAKES 16 ROLLS**

These delicious golden buns begin the magical time of Christmas, a glorious celebration of lights, family, and home. Bake a tray full for an early morning breakfast treat for your own Santa Lucia celebration.

1 tablespoon sugar
¼ cup warm water
1 package dry yeast (¼ ounce or 2 ¼ teaspoons)
½ cup salted butter
¾ cup milk
1 teaspoon saffron threads, chopped fine and soaked in a few drops of water
3 cups all-purpose flour
½ cup sugar
2 tablespoons vegetable oil (to grease bowl)
2 egg yolks, beaten with 1 tablespoon water
2 tablespoons raisins

Preheat oven to 400 degrees Fahrenheit. In the bowl of an electric mixer combine 1 tablespoon sugar, warm water, and yeast. Let sit for 10 minutes or until yeast begins to bubble and foam.

In a small saucepan combine butter, milk, and saffron. Heat until warm and butter is melted, but do not boil. Let sit for 8 minutes or until temperature falls below 110 degrees. Add milk mixture to yeast in the mixer bowl. Add flour and ½ cup sugar and beat with a dough hook until combined and the dough is smooth and workable; if necessary, add more flour 1 tablespoon at a time, up to 3 tablespoons. Turn dough out onto a lightly floured surface and knead for 1 minute. Transfer dough to a lightly oiled (or buttered) bowl, cover loosely with plastic food wrap, and let rise in a warm place for 1 hour. The dough will be dense and will not rise much.

Divide dough into 16 pieces. Roll each piece into 1-inch-wide, 6-inch-long strips. Coil ends in opposite directions, forming a tightly curled S-shape. Place on a baking sheet covered with Silpat liner (or parchment paper) and let rise for 1 hour more. Brush buns with beaten egg yolk and place 1 raisin in the center of each curl, 2 per bun. Bake until golden brown, about 10–15 minutes.

Fat Tuesday Buns

SEMLOR **MAKES 8 ROLLS**

Semlor are soft, sweet, fragrant buns filled with almond paste and luscious whipped cream. They are traditionally served during the cold, dark month of February in preparation for Lent and the fast. Often
served in a bowl of steaming milk, they warm your soul and body inside and out. These superdelicious
buns take me back to when I was twelve years old, my grandmother sat across the table, and the world
was full of possibilities.

3 tablespoons sugar, divided
¼ cup warm water
1 package dry yeast (¼ ounce or 2 ¼ teaspoons)
1 egg
½ cup heavy cream
¼ cup water
4 tablespoons salted butter
2 ½ cups all-purpose flour
1 egg yolk, beaten with 1 tablespoon cream (to brush on buns)

Filling:
½ cup premium almond paste, preferably Mandelin brand (¼ pound)
1 cup heavy whipping cream, beaten with 1 tablespoon sugar until soft peaks form
powdered sugar (to sprinkle on top)

Preheat oven to 400 degrees Fahrenheit. In a small bowl add 1 tablespoon sugar, warm water, and
yeast. Let sit for 10 minutes or until yeast begins to bubble and foam.

In the bowl of an electric mixer combine 2 tablespoons sugar and 1 egg and beat with whisk attachment until egg is pale, about 5 minutes.

In a small saucepan combine cream, water, and butter. Heat until warm and butter is melted, but do
not boil. Let sit for 8 minutes or until temperature falls below 110 degrees. Pour into the yeast mixture.

Add the yeast-cream mixture to the egg and stir to blend. Add flour and beat with dough hook until
dough forms; if necessary, add more flour 1 tablespoon at a time, up to 3 tablespoons. Turn dough
out on a lightly floured surface and knead for 1 minute. Transfer dough to a lightly oiled (or buttered)
bowl, cover loosely with plastic food wrap, and let rise in a warm place for 1 hour.

Divide dough into 8 pieces and roll into balls. Place on a baking sheet covered with Silpat liner (or
parchment paper) and let rise for 30 minutes more. Brush buns with beaten egg and cream mixture.
Bake until lightly browned, about 10–12 minutes. Let cool completely.

To fill the buns: Cut off the tops and scoop out a small part of the center. Fill with 1 tablespoon of almond paste and top with 1 heaping tablespoon of whipped cream. Place top over the whipped cream and dust with powdered sugar.

Serve in a bowl of warm milk with a spoon or on a plate with a dessert fork.

Note: Almond paste can be used full strength or it can be blended or thinned with the dough scooped from the center of the bun and a small amount of milk for a softer, milder texture and flavor. To make almond paste, grind ½ cup skinned almonds with ½ cup powdered sugar until fine. Add a small amount of raw egg white or cream to combine.

Bullar

BULLAR MAKES 16–18 ROLLS

Bullar is the staple, the magic, of Swedish fika. Eaten everywhere, this is the pastry that begins and ends the day. Served with coffee for adults and milk for children, bullar should always be eaten straight out of the oven.

My aunt was the star baker of bullar; no other bullar rivaled hers. I can close my eyes and smell bullar baking in her kitchen. My daughter spent three weeks in Sweden the summer she turned five, but today the only Swedish word she remembers in *bullar*.

1 teaspoon sugar
¼ cup warm water
1 package dry yeast (¼ ounce or 2 ¼ teaspoons)
¾ cup milk
¾ cup salted butter
1 egg
3 ¾ cups all-purpose flour
3 tablespoons sugar

Filling:
½ cup sugar
½ tablespoon ground cinnamon
1 teaspoon cardamom, ground fresh (page 139) or ½ teaspoon dry
4 tablespoons unsalted butter, softened at room temperature
1 egg, beaten (to brush the rolls)
pearl sugar or ½ cup powdered sugar, dissolved with 1 tablespoon water (for the topping)

In the bowl of an electric mixer, combine 1 teaspoon sugar, warm water, and yeast. Let sit for 10 minutes or until yeast begins to bubble and foam.

In a small saucepan combine milk and butter. Heat until warm and butter is melted, but do not boil. Let it sit for 8 minutes or until temperature falls below 110 degrees. Pour into the yeast mixture. Add egg, flour, and 3 tablespoons sugar and beat with a dough hook until combined. Turn dough out onto a floured surface and knead for 1 minute. Transfer dough to a lightly oiled (or buttered) bowl, cover loosely with plastic food wrap, and let rise in a warm place for 1 hour.

While the dough is rising, in a small bowl combine sugar, cinnamon, and cardamom. Preheat oven to 400 degrees Fahrenheit.

Roll dough into a 20 x 15-inch rectangle on a lightly floured surface. Brush top with the soft butter and evenly sprinkle with cinnamon sugar. Fold dough in half and cut into 1-inch-wide strips. Hold one end of each strip and twist in opposite directions. Coil the twisted strip around your finger to create a tightly rolled bun. Place inside paper muffin cups or on a baking sheet covered with a Silpat liner (or parchment paper). (Alternatively, bullar can be made jellyroll style, page 136, and cut into ½-inch sections.) Let rise in a warm place for 30 minutes more.

Brush rolls with the beaten egg and sprinkle with pearl sugar if desired, and bake for 10–12 minutes. (Alternatively, you can drizzle rolls with powdered-sugar glaze after they are baked.)

Sweet Rolls with Almond Paste

GIFFLAR **MAKES 16 ROLLS**

For a variation on bullar, the everyday pastry of Sweden (page 133), try these sweet rolls filled with almond paste.

3 tablespoons sugar, divided
¼ cup warm water
1 package dry yeast (¼ ounce or 2 ¼ teaspoons)
½ cup salted butter
1 egg
¼ cup half-and-half
2 cups all-purpose flour
1 ounce premium almond paste, preferably Mandelin brand
1 egg, beaten
pearl sugar and slivered almonds (to garnish)

In a small bowl combine 1 tablespoon of sugar, warm water, and yeast. Let sit for 8 minutes or until yeast begins to bubble and foam.

In the bowl of an electric mixer, cream butter with remaining 2 tablespoons sugar until light and fluffy, about 5 minutes. Add egg and mix until blended.

Stir proofed yeast, half-and-half, and flour into the mixer bowl until just combined and a soft, workable dough has formed; if necessary, add more flour 1 tablespoon at a time, up to 3 tablespoons. Wrap in plastic food wrap and let chill in the refrigerator for 1 hour.

Preheat oven to 400 degrees Fahrenheit. Cut dough into 2 equal pieces and roll each into a 10-inch circle. Cut each circle into 8 triangular wedges. With the wide end closest to you, place a small dollop (½ teaspoon) of almond paste near the bottom of the wedge. Roll up toward the pointy end, enclosing the paste. Continue until all of the wedges are rolled. Transfer rolls onto a baking sheet covered with a Silpat liner (or parchment paper) and let rise in a warm place for 30 minutes. Brush each roll with the beaten egg and sprinkle with pearl sugar and slivered almonds. Bake for 8–10 minutes.

Cinnamon Rolls

KAFFEBRÖD MED KANEL **MAKES 12 ROLLS**

Cinnamon and cardamom rolls are both variations of bullar. Cinnamon rolls are often generously studded with golden and dark raisins.

⅓ *cup plus 1 tablespoon sugar*
2 tablespoons warm water
1 package dry yeast (¼ ounce or 2 ¼ teaspoons)
1 cup unsalted butter, softened at room temperature
3 eggs
1 cup milk
4 ½ cups all-purpose flour
½ teaspoon salt

Filling:
4 tablespoons unsalted butter, softened at room temperature
⅓ cup sugar
1 tablespoon ground cinnamon
¾ cup golden raisins
¾ cup dark raisins

Glaze:
¼ cup sugar
¼ cup unsalted butter
¼ cup honey, maple syrup, or dark brown sugar
¼ cup heavy cream
⅓ cup slivered almonds

In a small bowl combine 1 tablespoon sugar, warm water, and yeast. Let sit for 8 minutes or until yeast begins to bubble and foam.

In the bowl of an electric mixer, cream the remaining sugar and butter until light and fluffy. Add eggs one at a time until fully incorporated.

In a small saucepan heat the milk until warm (below 110 degrees) and pour into yeast. Add the yeast-milk mixture to the mixer bowl. Stir in flour and salt and mix until well combined. Turn dough out onto a floured surface and knead for 1 minute. Transfer dough to a lightly oiled (or buttered) bowl, turn, cover loosely with plastic food wrap, and let rise in a warm place for 1 hour.

Preheat oven to 450 degrees Fahrenheit. Roll out dough on a floured surface into a large rectangle, about 20 x 15 inches. To prepare the filling, brush 4 tablespoons of butter over dough within half an inch of the edge. Sprinkle with sugar and cinnamon and evenly spread raisins over the dough.

Roll dough lengthwise, jellyroll style, enclosing the filling and creating a cylinder. Cut 1 ½-inch-thick sections to make 12 rolls. Transfer rolls onto a baking sheet covered with a Silpat liner (or parchment paper) and let rise for 30 minutes more. Bake for about 30 minutes.

To prepare the glaze, combine in a medium saucepan sugar, butter, honey, and cream and cook over low heat until light brown, about 5–8 minutes. Stir in almonds and set aside. Drizzle the tops of baked rolls with the almond/sugar mixture.

Cardamom Rolls

KAFFEBRÖD MED KARDEMUMMA MAKES 12 ROLLS

Cardamom is a favorite Scandinavian spice frequently used in baked goods. Fresh cardamom comes in three colors: green, white, and black. Green cardamom has the flavor and scent we commonly associate with this spice.

My grandmother would always grind fresh cardamom pods with a mortar and pestle. The magical fragrance would fill our kitchen when she baked these heavenly rolls.

1 tablespoon sugar
¼ cup warm water
1 package dry yeast (¼ ounce or 2 ¼ teaspoons)
¾ cup milk
1 tablespoon cream
½ cup unsalted butter
3 cups all-purpose flour
½ cup sugar
½ teaspoon salt
1 teaspoon freshly ground cardamom

Filling:
2 tablespoons unsalted butter, softened at room temperature
3 tablespoons sugar
½ teaspoon cinnamon

Topping:
1 egg, beaten
slivered almonds and pearl sugar (to garnish)

In the bowl of an electric mixer, add 1 tablespoon sugar, warm water, and yeast. Let sit for 10 minutes or until yeast begins to bubble and foam.

In a small saucepan combine milk, cream, and butter. Heat until warm and butter is melted, but do not boil. Let sit for 8 minutes or until temperature falls below 110 degrees. Pour into the yeast mixture and blend.

In a medium bowl combine flour, sugar, salt, and cardamom. Stir into the liquid batter and mix. Knead dough by hand for 1 minute. Transfer dough to a lightly oiled (or buttered) bowl covered loosely with plastic food wrap. Let rise in a warm place for 1 hour.

Preheat oven to 400 degrees Fahrenheit.

On a floured surface, roll out the dough to a quarter-inch-thick rectangle (16 x 18 inches). Spread the softened butter in a thin layer over the dough and evenly sprinkle with sugar and cinnamon.

Roll the dough jellyroll style and cut into 1 ½-inch-thick sections. Place on a baking sheet covered with a Silpat liner (or parchment paper). Let rise for 30 minutes more. Brush with beaten egg and sprinkle with slivered almonds and pearl sugar. Bake for 10–12 minutes.

Note: Before grinding cardamom, remove the green pods by crushing them with a rolling pin (or whirling them a few times in a food processor). Scrape out seeds and discard pods. Grind seeds using a mortar and pestle or a food processor. The seeds do not need to be ground fine; they should be small and coarse.

Apple-Cranberry Coffeecake

ÄPPELKAKA SERVES 6

For an alternative to a standard apple pie, try this beautiful and fragrant coffeecake filled with apples, cranberries, cardamom, and cinnamon.

4 tablespoons sugar, divided
¼ cup water
1 package dry yeast (¼ ounce or 2 ¼ teaspoons)
1 egg, beaten
¼ cup unsalted butter
¾ cup milk
1 teaspoon salt
3 ¼ cups all-purpose flour

Filling:
2 apples, peeled and shredded fine
1 tablespoon fresh lemon juice
3 tablespoons sugar
¼ teaspoon ground cardamom
¼ teaspoon ground cinnamon
½ cup dried cranberries, raisins, or currants
1 egg, beaten (to brush over cake)

Glaze:
½ cup powdered sugar
½ tablespoon water

In the bowl of an electric mixer, combine 1 tablespoon of sugar, warm water, and yeast. Let sit for 10 minutes or until yeast begins to bubble and foam. Add beaten egg to yeast mix.

In a small saucepan combine butter and milk. Heat until warm and butter is melted, but do not boil. Add remaining sugar and salt. Let sit for 8 minutes or until temperature falls below 110 degrees. Pour milk and butter into yeast mixture and add flour. Mix until combined and dough is well blended. Turn dough out onto a floured surface and knead for 1 minute. Transfer dough to a lightly oiled (or buttered) bowl, cover with plastic food wrap, and let rise in a warm place for 30 minutes.

While the dough is rising, prepare the filling. In a medium bowl combine apples, lemon juice, 3 table-spoons sugar, cardamom, cinnamon, and cranberries.

Preheat oven to 400 degrees Fahrenheit.

Roll dough into a long rectangle (15 x 8 inches) and lay it on a baking sheet covered with a Silpat liner (or parchment paper). Spread filling down the center of the dough, leaving any accumulated juices in the bowl. Fold sides of the dough to enclose the filling (like a burrito), then seal both ends. Using scissors, snip cuts left, right, and center all the way up the dough, creating decorative slits. Let cake rise for 30 minutes more. Brush with beaten egg and bake for 20 minutes.

While the cake is baking, prepare the glaze by mixing the water with the powdered sugar. When done, remove cake from oven and drizzle with glaze. Cut into 2-inch-wide slices for serving.

Dream Cookies

DRÖMMAR **MAKES 30 COOKIES**

Sweet butter cooked until golden brown, similar to caramel in color and scent, is the main flavor in dream cookies.

As the cookie crumbles in your mouth, you dream of Swedish summers, basking in the midnight sun in the middle of a meadow, surrounded by wildflowers.

To achieve the full glory of summer, serve dream cookies with berry juice (page 158).

1 cup unsalted butter
1 cup sugar
½ teaspoon vanilla extract or 2 teaspoons vanilla sugar
2 cups all-purpose flour
2 teaspoons baking powder

In a small, heavy skillet fry butter over low heat until brown, about 5 minutes. The butter will foam as it is cooking; it is done when it looks and smells like caramel. Remove from heat before it overcooks and becomes bitter. Transfer butter to a small bowl and set in a larger bowl filled with ice to cool.

Transfer cooled butter to the bowl of an electric mixer, add sugar, and beat until light and fluffy. Add vanilla, flour, and baking powder and stir until just combined. The mixture will be very crumbly. Transfer dough to a large sheet of plastic food wrap and form into a log. (If the dough will not hold together to form a log, knead in 1 additional tablespoon of uncooked butter.) Let chill in the refrigerator 1 hour.

Preheat oven to 300 degrees Fahrenheit. Cut dough into pieces, form small balls, and place on baking sheet covered with Silpat liner (or parchment paper). Bake 15 minutes. Let cool before serving.

Whiskey Gingersnaps

PEPPARKAKOR   MAKES 100 ULTRATHIN COOKIES

Pepparkakor are served throughout the holiday season and are always part of a Santa Lucia tray. These ginger cookies can be made by combining all of the ingredients in a mixing bowl, but I prefer to cook the spices with the sugar so that the ginger, cardamom, and cinnamon infuse the kitchen with the magical scent of Christmas to welcome my guests. I can still remember my grandmother stirring the fragrant mixture. After she added the butter, I would lick the spoon and sneak a taste of the warm, sweet batter when she was not watching.

1 ½ cups sugar
½ cup water
¼ cup maple syrup, molasses, or dark corn syrup
½ tablespoon ground cinnamon
½ tablespoon ground ginger
1 teaspoon ground cardamom
½ teaspoon ground cloves
1 tablespoon whiskey
¾ cup salted butter, cut into small pieces
4 ½ cups all-purpose flour
2 teaspoons baking soda

In a medium-heavy saucepan combine sugar, water, syrup, cinnamon, ginger, cardamom, and cloves. Heat over gentle flame until sugar dissolves or until the fragrance of the spices has been released, about 5 minutes. Stir in whiskey and let cool for 5 minutes. Transfer sugar mixture to the bowl of an electric mixer and add butter pieces gradually. Blend well. Add flour and baking soda. Wrap dough in plastic food wrap and let it cool in the refrigerator for 2 hours or until the next day.

Preheat oven to 400 degrees Fahrenheit.

Cut dough into thirds. On a lightly floured surface roll out pieces, one section at a time, until they are very thin. Cut with a cookie cutter and transfer onto a baking sheet covered with a Silpat liner (or parchment paper). Bake for 10 minutes. This recipe makes 100 ultrathin cookies—if you do not consume too much of the dough, that is.

Pearl Sugar Cookies

KARL XV:S KAKOR MAKES 26–30 COOKIES

Pearl sugar cookies are made simply by combining flour, butter, and a sprinkling of cream. The cookies are then topped generously with pearl sugar.

These cookies must be made with sweet butter, as the dough itself does not have sugar in it. The quality of the sweet butter will make a big difference in the taste of the cookie.

12 tablespoons sweet butter (¾ cup), preferably Plugra
3 tablespoons buttermilk or cream
1 ¼ cups all-purpose flour
¼ teaspoon grated lemon peel
1 egg, beaten
½ cup pearl sugar

In the bowl of an electric mixer beat butter until smooth, about 2 minutes. Add buttermilk and beat until combined. Stir in flour and lemon peel and beat until just combined. Wrap dough tightly in a large sheet of plastic food wrap and chill in the refrigerator for 1 hour.

Preheat oven to 400 degrees Fahrenheit. Roll out dough on a floured surface, turning at least once, until it is about ¼-inch thick. Cut with a cookie cutter and transfer cookies to a baking sheet covered with a Silpat liner (or parchment paper). Brush with beaten egg and sprinkle generously with pearl sugar. Bake for 10 minutes. Cool before eating.

Swedish Cheesecake

OSTKAKA **SERVES 6**

Swedish cheesecake is similar to Italian-style ricotta cheesecake, except that the Swedish version does not have a crust and does not include vanilla or lemon.

If this sounds bland, think again: this is the perfect sweet and mellow treat to serve with fresh berries. Spoon ripe cloudberries, currants, and blueberries over the cake, then top it all with a generous serving of sweetened whipped cream. Finish it with a dusting of powdered sugar—a simply glorious dessert.

2 eggs
4 tablespoons all-purpose flour
1 ½ cups half-and-half
½ cup blanched almonds, chopped fine
1 container whole-milk ricotta or cottage cheese (15 ounces)
2 tablespoons sugar

Preheat oven to 350 degrees Fahrenheit. In a large bowl whisk eggs, flour, and half-and-half. Stir in almonds, cheese, and sugar. Whisk until well combined. Pour into a greased, 1 ½-quart bread loaf pan and bake for 1 hour. Serve chilled with fresh berries and whipped cream.

Three-Berry Birthday Cake

FÖDELSEDAGSTÅRTA MED JORDGUBBAR SERVES 8

The most popular Swedish birthday cake is a simple white cake overflowing with ripe blueberries, straw-berries, raspberries, and bananas. It is filled and garnished with sweetened whipped cream. You can use any basic white cake recipe or the one below.

I never had a big birthday party while growing up, but my grandmother would make a beautiful three-berry cake for me every year. My friends Monica and Pia would come over. Our mismatched trio made up the "freak and geek" section of our class.

No matter how old I was, we would place as many candles on the cake as it could possibly hold. I would close my eyes, take a deep breath, and blow out the candles after making a wish: that my friends and I would no longer be geeks but be cool. But as I ate that marvelous cake, with its juicy berries and whipped cream, and as I laughed with my grandmother and friends, I realized I did not want to be cool. I was exactly what I wanted to be.

Basic White Cake:
1 cup unsalted butter
2 cups sugar
4 eggs
1 cup plain original kefir (or buttermilk)
1 teaspoon vanilla extract
½ teaspoon almond extract
3 cups cake flour
⅛ teaspoon baking soda
⅛ teaspoon baking powder
⅛ teaspoon salt
2 teaspoons lemon peel

Filling:
2 pints strawberries, hulled
2 tablespoons sugar
1 tablespoon fresh lemon juice
4 bananas, sliced thin
2 pints blueberries
2 pints raspberries
2 cups heavy cream, whipped with 2 tablespoons sugar
  and 1 tablespoon vanilla extract until medium soft peaks form

Preheat oven to 325 degrees Fahrenheit. Butter and flour a 10-inch round springform cake pan (with removable sides). In the bowl of an electric mixer cream butter and sugar until light and fluffy. Add eggs one at a time until fully incorporated. Add kefir and extracts, then flour, baking soda, baking powder, salt, and lemon peel and stir until just combined. Pour into pan and bake until a toothpick inserted in the center comes out dry, about 55–60 minutes.

While cake is baking, cut most of the strawberries into thin slices; leave about 1 cup of berries whole for garnish. Combine sliced strawberries with 2 tablespoons of sugar and lemon juice; set aside.

Let cake cool completely. Remove sides from the pan. Using a thin, long serrated knife, slice cake horizontally into three layers, each about half an inch thick. Transfer the bottom layer to a serving platter and spread half of the sliced strawberries over the layer, letting the accumulated juices soak the cake. On top of the strawberries spread half of the sliced bananas, one-third of the blueberries, and one-third of the raspberries. Top the fruit with a thin layer of whipped cream. Place second layer of cake on top and cover with remaining sliced strawberries and bananas, and the second third of the blueberries and raspberries. Top with a second thin layer of whipped cream and cover with the top layer of cake. Spread remaining whipped cream over the top and sides of cake. Use a pastry bag to decoratively pipe on additional cream.

Garnish the cake with reserved whole strawberries and remaining third of the blueberries and raspberries.

Cloudberry Shortcakes

SMÅKAKOR MED HJORTRON **MAKES 10 SHORTCAKES**

These shortcakes can be filled with any seasonal berries. They also can be served warm, spread with butter or berry preserve (page 173–78).

Shortcakes:
1 ¾ cups all-purpose flour
2 ½ teaspoons baking powder
1 ¼ teaspoons salt
2 tablespoons sugar
¼ cup unsalted butter, cut into small pieces
¾ cup milk
2 tablespoons heavy cream
4 tablespoons powdered sugar

Filling:
2 cups cloudberries or other berries, such as strawberries
2 tablespoons sugar
2 tablespoons orange juice
1 teaspoon fresh orange zest
1 cup heavy whipping cream, whipped with 2 tablespoons of sugar
    and ½ tablespoon vanilla extract until soft peaks form
powdered sugar (to dust cooked cakes)

Preheat oven to 425 degrees Fahrenheit. Place flour, baking powder, salt, and sugar in the bowl of a food processor. Pulse briefly, add butter gradually and the milk, and pulse until just combined. Turn out onto a floured surface and knead for 1 minute. Roll dough out to a 1-inch-thick rectangle and cut into 2-inch rounds using a cookie cutter. Transfer cut rounds to a baking sheet covered with a Silpat liner (or parchment paper), brush with cream, and sprinkle with powdered sugar. Bake 10–12 minutes. Remove cakes from the oven and let cool before serving.

While cakes are baking, make the filling. Combine cloudberries (or other berries) with the sugar, orange juice, and orange zest. Set aside.

To serve the shortcakes, cut them in half horizontally and divide fruit evenly among bottom halves, including any accumulated juices. Top fruit with a generous tablespoon of whipped cream. Place top of the shortcake over the cream and dust with powdered sugar.

Flourless Meyer Lemon Apple Cake with Vanilla Sauce

ÄPPELKAKA MED VANILJKRÄM SERVES 6

Although these individual apple cakes are delicious at room temperature, they will fall like soufflés shortly after baking. It is best to serve them straight from the oven, when they are puffy and golden.

Apple Cakes:
2 green apples, peeled, cored, and chopped fine
juice from 1 Meyer (sweet) lemon (3 tablespoons)
½ cup salted butter
½ cup sugar
3 egg yolks
¾ cup almonds, ground fine in a spice mill or food processor
3 egg whites, whipped to stiff peaks
powdered sugar (for dusting)

Vanilla Sauce:
1 vanilla bean, cut in half lengthwise
¾ cup heavy cream
2 egg yolks
2 tablespoons sugar

Preheat oven to 400 degrees Fahrenheit. Butter six ¾-cup ramekins. Toss apples with lemon juice, divide into six equal portions, and place in the bottom of each dish.

In the bowl of an electric mixer beat butter and sugar until light and fluffy, about 2 minutes. Add egg yolks one at a time until incorporated. Fold in almonds and egg whites. Spread batter over the apples, up to the top of ramekins. Bake in preheated oven for 15–20 minutes.

While cakes are baking, prepare the vanilla sauce. Into a small, heavy saucepan scrape the seeds from the vanilla bean, add cream, and cook both seeds and pod for 1 minute. Let steep for 10 minutes, then remove and discard the pod.

In the bowl of an electric mixer, beat egg yolks with sugar until thick and pale yellow, about 5 minutes. With the motor running on low, slowly pour in the warm cream until fully incorporated. Return to the saucepan and simmer, whisking constantly until slightly thickened, about 5–8 minutes more.

To serve, poke a hole in the center of each baked cake and pour in a small amount of vanilla sauce. Garnish with powdered sugar and serve immediately.

Rice Pudding à la Malta

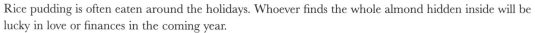

RIS À LA MALTA MED SAFTSÅS SERVES 4-6

Rice pudding is often eaten around the holidays. Whoever finds the whole almond hidden inside will be lucky in love or finances in the coming year.

Rice pudding flavored with oranges is called ris à la Malta. As I was growing up, the exotic foreign name made me dream of faraway lands and travels.

Creamy, rich, and sweet, rice pudding is traditionally served with a wild berry sauce, made by adding 1 tablespoon of thickener (such as cornstarch) to 1 cup of berry juice (page 158).

Rice:
1 cup short-grain white rice
½ cup fresh orange juice
½ cup heavy cream
1 cup water
1 tablespoon sugar
pinch of saffron
1 whole cinnamon stick

Pudding:
½ cup dark raisins
½ cup rum
1 cup heavy cream, whipped with 1 tablespoon sugar
    and 1 tablespoon of vanilla extract until it holds soft peaks form
2 oranges, peeled and cut into small sections
1 whole almond (optional)

In a medium saucepan combine rice, orange juice, cream, water, sugar, saffron, and cinnamon stick. Bring to a boil and cook according to package instructions, about 15 minutes. Remove from heat, cover, and let steam for 15 minutes. Transfer to a bowl and let cool.

While the rice is cooling, bring raisins and rum to a gentle boil for 1 minute. Remove from heat, and let raisins absorb some of the rum.

Fold whipped cream, oranges, raisins, and the whole almond, if desired, into the rice. Serve with fresh berry sauce (page 158) or use in rice pudding crème brûlée (page 151).

Rice Pudding Crème Brûlée

CRÈME BRÛLÉE SERVES 8

2 ½ cups heavy cream
8 large egg yolks
1 cup sugar
1 tablespoon vanilla extract
1 cup Rice Pudding (page 150)

Preheat oven to 325 degrees Fahrenheit. In a medium saucepan bring cream to a low simmer for 2 minutes. Remove from heat and set aside.

In the bowl of an electric mixer, combine egg yolks and ½ cup sugar until light and fluffy, about 5 minutes. With mixer on low, add warm cream and vanilla.

Place 1 heaping tablespoon of rice pudding in the bottom of eight ¾-cup ramekins. Divide evenly and pour crème brûlée mixture over pudding. Place ramekins in the bottom of a large roasting pan and fill pan with 1 inch of warm water. Bake for 20 minutes. Cool completely in the refrigerator. After they are fully cooled, spread a thin layer (1 tablespoon) of sugar over each crème brûlée. Using a blow torch or a hot broiler, melt the sugar until caramelized to a deep brown.

Rhubarb Crisp

RABABERPAJ SERVES 4–6

In this recipe, rhubarb and apples are covered with a crunchy topping and baked until the tart, crisp rhubarb turns sweet and soft.

1 ½ pounds Granny Smith apples, peeled, cored, and cut into chunks
1 pound rhubarb, coarse ends trimmed and discarded, stalks cut into 1-inch pieces
juice (¼ cup) and zest (1 tablespoon) from 1 orange
1 cup brown sugar, firmly packed
½ teaspoon ground cinnamon
⅛ teaspoon ground cloves
2 teaspoons fresh ginger, minced
¾ cup plus 2 tablespoons all-purpose flour
¼ cup pecans
½ cup sugar
6 tablespoons salted butter

Garnish:
1 cup whipping cream
1 tablespoon powdered sugar
1 teaspoon vanilla extract

Preheat oven to 375 degrees. In a 3-quart baking dish, combine apples, rhubarb, orange juice and zest, brown sugar, cinnamon, cloves, ginger, and 2 tablespoons flour. Mix well. In a food processor, combine ¾ cup flour, pecans, and sugar, and whirl until nuts are ground fine. Add butter and whirl until mixture forms fine crumbs. Squeeze crumbs into lumps and scatter over apple-rhubarb mixture. Bake until topping is well browned and juice bubbles at edges, about 40 minutes.

While the rhubarb crisp is baking, in a chilled bowl whip cream on high speed with powdered sugar and vanilla until it holds soft peaks. Let crisp cool for a few minutes before serving with the whipped cream.

Soft Rye Bread

LIMPA **MAKES 2 LOAVES**

Rye flour is very popular in Sweden, used for making both soft and crisp bread (page 154). Rye bread is best served straight out of the oven or toasted with sweet butter. The bread can be made with or without raisins.

1 teaspoon honey
¼ cup warm water
2 packages dry yeast (¼ ounce each or 4 ½ teaspoons total)
¾ cup milk
4 tablespoons sweet or salted butter (2 ounces)
1 cup dark beer
1 teaspoon salt
¼ cup maple syrup
½ tablespoon ground cumin
3 ¼ cups rye flour
2 ½ cups all-purpose flour
1 cup golden raisins (optional)
1 cup dark raisins (optional)

Preheat oven to 350 degrees Fahrenheit. In the bowl of an electric mixer add honey, warm water, and yeast. Let sit for 10 minutes or until yeast begins to bubble and foam.

In a medium saucepan heat milk over low heat, add butter, and stir until melted. Add beer. Pour milk mixture into the yeast mixture and add salt, syrup, cumin, rye flour, and all-purpose flour. Stir in raisins if desired. Beat until combined. The dough will be fairly stiff. Transfer dough to a lightly oiled (or buttered) bowl, sprinkle with flour, and cover with plastic food wrap. Let rise in a warm place for 30 minutes.

Grease two 1 ½-quart loaf pans. Turn dough out onto a lightly floured surface and knead until glossy, about 2 minutes. Divide dough into two loaves and place into prepared pans. Let rise in a warm place for 30 more minutes. Brush loaves with water and sprinkle lightly with flour. Bake for 30 minutes.

Swedish Crisp Bread

KNÄCKEBRÖD MAKES 16 CRISP BREADS

Swedish crisp bread is eaten with almost every meal, from breakfast to dinner. There are dozens of varieties of crisp bread in Sweden, usually known as *wasa*. It is eaten plain or spread with a thin layer of butter and with assorted sandwich toppings such as sliced cheese and pickles. *Wasa* can be bought at most well-stocked supermarkets.

1 teaspoon sugar
2 cups warm water, divided
2 packages dry yeast (¼ ounce each or 4 ½ teaspoons total)
1 ½ teaspoons salt
3 ½ cups rye flour
1 ½ cups all-purpose flour
olive oil spray

In the bowl of an electric mixer add sugar, ¼ cup warm water, and yeast. Let sit for 10 minutes or until yeast begins to bubble and foam. Stir in remaining water, salt, rye flour, and all-purpose flour. Beat with dough hook until well combined, about 5 minutes. Transfer dough to a lightly oiled (or buttered) bowl, sprinkle with flour, and cover with plastic food wrap. Let rise in the refrigerator overnight.

Preheat oven to 350 degrees Fahrenheit. Divide dough into 16 pieces. On a floured surface, roll each piece into a thin, 8-inch round. Poke out a small, ¼-inch center hole and poke the round all over with a fork. Brush off excess flour, spray with olive oil on both sides, and transfer to a baking sheet covered with a Silpat liner (or parchment paper). Bake 10–15 minutes. Let cool before serving.

NOTES

Beverages

The most important beverage custom in Sweden is that of skål. The usually reserved Swedes become downright sociable after one or two schnapps, the ultimate icebreaker.

Skål is traditionally done with schnapps, and often with any form of alcohol (except wine). As the evening progresses, however, all bets are off.

The main difference between skål and a toast is that even the most shy, most inarticulate person will gladly and frequently skål. The only thing that needs to be said is that simple four-letter word. During a toast a person is usually expected to say at least a few charming and funny words about the occasion or the host.

In Sweden alcohol is expensive and can be purchased only in government-run stores, where long lines form on weekends. Swedes stand in orderly lines, patiently awaiting their turn. They wait everywhere, from the bank to the post office.

The preferred nonalcoholic drinks in Sweden are juices made from fresh berries such as cranberry, blueberry, and gooseberry. Combined with sugar, water, and lemon, the juices make sweet, slightly tangy drinks. Most juices are made by steeping the berries in water and sugar and allowing the natural flavor of the perfectly ripe berries to shine through before being chilled and consumed. The berry juices bring the magic of the forest floor into a glass.

Berry Juice

SAFT MAKES 1 QUART

Before they reach the age of skål, Swedish children drink a popular beverage called saft, which is made of the ripest seasonal berries. This refreshing drink brings home the flavors of summer. A typical snack on a Swedish summer day is bullar (page 133) and saft while basking in the glory of the sun.

1 quart water
4 ½ cups mixed berries (strawberries, raspberries, blueberries)
1 cup sugar

In a medium stockpot bring water and berries to a boil over medium heat, and cook for 10 minutes. With an immersion blender (or a conventional blender), process berries until crushed. Drain through a mesh strainer lined with cheesecloth; discard solids. Transfer juice back to the pot, add sugar, and bring to a simmer over low heat until the sugar dissolves. Transfer to a glass (or plastic) pitcher, cover with plastic food wrap, and let cool in the refrigerator. Serve over ice.

Strawberry-Papaya Juice

JORDGUBBS OCH PAPAYASAFT MAKES 1 QUART

Sweet fruit juices can be simply prepared and served straight out of the blender, or cooked and then chilled. Either way the juice is refreshing and delicious. Use only the freshest and perfectly ripe berries to make berry drinks.

1 pint strawberries, hulled and sliced
1 small papaya, peeled, seeded, and cut into chunks
¾ cup sugar
2 cups water
½ cup fresh lemon juice

Purée all ingredients in a blender. Serve straight out of the blender over ice.

For a sweeter, more syrupy flavor, cook in a medium saucepan for 5 minutes and chill before serving. The juice will separate when left sitting; stir to combine before serving.

Blueberry Lemonade

BLÅBÄRSDRICKA MAKES 4 CUPS

Fresh blueberry juice is tangy and sweet. It is terrific served over vanilla ice cream.

2 pints blueberries
⅓ cup to ½ cup sugar
2 cups water
½ cup fresh lemon juice

Purée all ingredients in a blender. Chill and serve over ice or vanilla ice cream.

Gooseberry Juice

KRUSBÄRSDRICKA MAKES 4 CUPS

Gooseberry juice has an amazing flavor. Its sweetness is mellow and refreshing with a hint of tartness. A glass of gooseberry juice for breakfast is the beginning of a beautiful day.

2 cups ripe yellow Sweet Cape gooseberries, with tough outer husks removed
¼ cup sugar
1 ½ cups water
1 tablespoon lemon juice

In a blender purée all ingredients. Transfer to a container and let steep overnight in the refrigerator. In a fine mesh strainer, strain out and discard the solids, reserving the juice. Chill and serve.

Note: Do not replace Sweet Cape gooseberries with the more commonly available green groseilles vertes *variety. The green gooseberries are too tart to be suitable for juice.*

Fresh Cranberry Juice

LINGONDRICKA MAKES 1 QUART

This fresh, simple, healthy juice is easy to make and has a glorious ruby-red color. Cranberry juice is frequently served as a lunch drink in Sweden.

4 cups cranberries
3 cups water, divided
1 tablespoon fresh lemon juice
1 cup sugar

In a blender or food processor, blend cranberries with 2 cups of water and lemon juice. Let steep in the refrigerator overnight. Drain through a fine mesh strainer and discard the solids. Transfer mixture to a medium saucepan and heat over medium heat. Add sugar and cook until the sugar is completely dissolved, about 1 minute. Add 1 cup cold water (or more, to taste) and chill before serving.

Strawberry-Rhubarb Juice

JORDGUBBS OCH RABARBERDRICKA MAKES 6 QUARTS

Using rhubarb from her little backyard patch, my aunt would make batches of sweet, tart, and delicious rhubarb juice. The juice can be made with rhubarb only, but to reduce the amount of sugar it is best to add either strawberries or raspberries to the juice.

2 pounds rhubarb, tough ends removed and discarded and stalks cut into 1-inch sections
1 pint strawberries, hulled and sliced
1 pint raspberries
6 quarts water
1 cup sugar

In a large stockpot combine rhubarb, berries, and water. Bring to a boil over medium heat, and let simmer for 10 minutes. Using an immersion blender (or after transferring mix to a conventional blender in batches), process fruit until smooth. Drain through a mesh strainer lined with cheesecloth and discard the solids. Return berry liquid to the pot and stir in sugar; return to a low simmer until sugar is dissolved, about 1–2 minutes. Transfer to a glass or plastic pitcher and let cool in the refrigerator. Serve over ice.

Glogg

GLÖGG MAKES 2 QUARTS

During gatherings of family and friends throughout the Christmas season, this hot spiced wine drink is found simmering on the stove.

1 bottle dry red wine
½ bottle port wine
½ cup vodka
½ cup aquavit (page 165)
peel from 1 orange
1 cinnamon stick
6 whole cardamom seeds, lightly crushed
¼ cup sugar
¼ cup whole blanched almonds
½ cup raisins

In a large pot, combine all ingredients except sugar, almonds, and raisins, and let sit for 1 hour. Over low heat, bring mixture to a low simmer but do not boil. Stir in sugar, almonds, and raisins. Serve hot.

Aquavit

AQUAVIT   MAKES 1 QUART

Aquavit comes from the Latin phrase *aqua vitae*—the water of life, or the essence of all good things in life. Aquavit should be served ice cold in a small shot glass and drunk in a single gulp. Skål!

rind from 1 orange
rind from 1 lemon
rind from 1 lime
1 teaspoon fennel seeds
1 teaspoon caraway seeds
1 bottle vodka (Absolut)

Add citrus rinds and spices to vodka in a clean 1-quart bottle or glass pitcher. Let it marinate for 3 days. Strain, chill, and serve.

Rose Hips Tea

NYPONTE **MAKES 5 CUPS**

Dried rose hips can be used to make soup (page 4) or a simple and soothing hot herb tea. Rose hips are available in most well-stocked health-food stores and gourmet markets.

1 cup dried rose hips
5 cups cold water
1 tablespoon sugar (optional)
1 lemon, cut into wedges (optional)

In a small saucepan combine 1 cup of rose hips with water. Bring to a simmer over medium heat for 5 minutes. Turn off heat, cover, and let steep for 2 minutes more. Strain and discard rose hips. Serve hot as is or add sugar and lemon.

To serve as iced tea, stir in sugar and squeeze in lemon juice or leave whole wedges in the tea. Chill and serve over ice.

Nettle Herb Tea

TE PÅ NÄSSLOR MAKES 6 CUPS

Dried nettles make great "green" tea. To dry fresh nettles, hang them upside down in a dark and dry room until completely dry, about one week.

6 cups water
1 bunch fresh (or dried) nettles
sugar to taste (optional)
thin lemon slices (optional)

Bring water to a boil. Stir in fresh or dried nettles (tea made with dried nettles will remain green). Turn off the heat, cover, and let steep for 5 minutes. Serve hot as is or add sugar and lemon.

To serve as iced tea, stir in sugar and lemon slices. Chill and serve over ice.

Chamomile Tea

ÖRTTE   MAKES 6 CUPS

Tea made from the daisylike chamomile flower is considered soothing, calming, and rejuvenating. Chamomile tea is quick and easy to make and can be steeped from fresh or dried chamomile.

6 cups water
1 bunch fresh (or dried) chamomile
½ bunch purple basil (optional)
sugar to taste (optional)
thin slices of lemon (optional)

Bring water to a boil and add herbs. Turn off heat, cover, and let steep for 5 minutes. Strain herbs and serve tea as is or with sugar and lemon.

For iced tea, stir in sugar and lemon slices. Chill and serve over ice.

NOTES

Wild Berry Preserves

While growing up in Sweden, I never smelled fresh pineapple, tasted a fresh peach, or felt the smoothness of an avocado. But I did know the wild berries of the forest floor. The tiny summerhouse my grandfather built by the lake's edge was hidden deep in the magical forest in the north of Sweden. At the end of the summer, bucket in hand, I would walk into the forest with my grandmother. As we followed the tiny trail, the forest became denser, darker, and more quiet. Then, around the bend, light filtered through the branches into a clearing. To the untrained eye, the forest floor was just that: the floor of the forest. But to the treasure hunter who carefully looked down, that clearing was rich in wild berries that sparkled like jewels in the sunlight.

Although in her late seventies, my grandmother would bend, kneel, and pick berries that would slowly but surely fill her bucket to the rim. I would continue my way past her to a point where she could no longer see me. Then I would sit, a tiny figure among the giant trees, and pop the berries in my mouth, none making it into my basket. After a while I could hear my grandmother calling me, and I would come out, shaking my head, showing her my empty bucket, telling her there were no berries over where I had been looking. She would smile because my berry-stained lips and hands betrayed me. Hand in hand we would walk back to our tiny house to eat berries with sprinkled sugar and whipped cream, and to make preserves to last us through the long winter months.

The Swedish forest floor offers a wide variety of berries, some of which are available in the United States. Tart cloudberries are raspberry-shaped, amber-colored treasures that are soft but crunchy with little seeds inside. *Smultron* are tiny wild strawberries, dense and much sweeter than regular strawberries. Lingonberries are small, sweeter, yet more tart and a deeper red than the cranberries in America. Blueberries, currants (mostly red), and gooseberries are also widely available.

When we pulled up to our little cottage the summer I was fourteen, my heart nearly stopped. The forest surrounding the summerhouse, the magic place of my childhood, had been clear-cut. Some mature trees had been left and saplings planted in their place, but the forest was essentially gone. I knew summers would never be the same.

Ten years later, I returned with my young daughter and husband to show them the Sweden of my childhood. In the same 1968 Volkswagen bug I had traveled in as a child, we cruised down the highway to the summerhouse. My heart beat faster as we approached, and then around the bend I could see it: the forest was back. Maybe it was not as dense or the trees were not as high, but the tiny cottage was surrounded by trees once again, completely sheltered from the road. Everything else had changed, too, of course. My grandmother had long since passed away, and my favorite aunt, the master chef of Swedish fika, would soon succumb to cancer. But as I walked into the forest to pick berries, holding my daughter's hand, I knew that she was the beginning of a new generation. I knew that with time, everything would change again, yet everything would stay the same.

For the first time, my daughter picked a basket full of glorious red and golden berries. We returned to the little cottage by the water and continued the Swedish tradition of making tangy-sweet preserves with freshly picked berries, and of spreading them thickly on toasted country bread with sweet butter, as we watched the midnight sun hovering just above the horizon.

Cloudberry Preserve

RÅRÖRD HJORTRONSYLT

Cloudberries grow wild in the Swedish forest as well as in New England and Canada. They look like amber-colored raspberries but are not to be confused with the golden raspberry; they are more tart, and their small seeds crunch as you bite into them. Because they usually grow wild, they are difficult to find in markets.

Cloudberries make excellent jam and preserves and are especially delicious spread on buttered toast or on shortcakes (page 148).

4 cups cloudberries or raspberries, strawberries, or other available berry
¾ cup sugar
1 tablespoon fresh lemon juice

Gently combine all ingredients in a medium-size bowl. Let sit until berries and sugar begin to combine and juices are released.

The preserve keeps for one week in the refrigerator.

Raspberry Preserve

HALLONSYLT

Fresh raspberry preserve is excellent on toast and biscuits. Raspberries grow wild in the forest in the north of Sweden but are also planted and grown in backyard gardens.

4 cups raspberries
½ cup red currants
½ cup sugar
1 tablespoon fresh lemon juice

Combine all ingredients in a small, heavy saucepan. Cook over low heat for 30 minutes, stirring occasionally. Cool to room temperature before using.

The preserve keeps for one week in the refrigerator.

Gooseberry Preserve

KRUSBÄRSSYLT

Gooseberries are tart yet sweet berries that grow on bushes and come in different varieties, including yellow, red, and white. They make excellent jam and jellies, and their tart flavor makes them a superb addition to salads (page 87) and/or other savory dishes. This preserve is great on toasted country bread with sweet butter or goat cheese.

4 cups ripe yellow Sweet Cape gooseberries, with tough outer husks removed
¾ cup sugar
1 tablespoon fresh lemon juice

Combine all ingredients in a small, heavy saucepan. Cook over low heat for 30 minutes, stirring occasionally. Cool to room temperature before using.

The preserve keeps for one week in the refrigerator.

Note: In this recipe, the yellow Sweet Cape gooseberries can be replaced with the more commonly available green groseilles vertes *variety. The green gooseberries make a much tarter but still delicious preserve.*

Strawberry Preserve
JORDGUBBSSYLT

The ingredients for berry preserves can be combined and cooked immediately (as in the preceding recipes), or the berries and sugar can be allowed to macerate first, infusing the sugar into the berries, which creates a deep, syrupy jam.

4 cups strawberries, hulled
¾ cups sugar
2 tablespoons fresh lemon juice

Slice strawberries in half and in a large bowl combine with sugar and lemon juice. Let mixture sit at room temperature until juices are released, about 30 minutes. Combine all ingredients in a small, heavy saucepan. Cook over low heat, stirring occasionally, until slightly thickened, about 45–60 minutes. Remove foam from the surface with a spoon. Cool to room temperature before using.

The preserve keeps for one week in the refrigerator.

Blood Orange Preserve

BLODAPELSINMARMELAD

This bittersweet preserve remains spectacularly dark red after cooking. Spread on toasted country bread with sweet butter or on hot croissants.

4 blood oranges, quartered and sliced very thin
4 cups water
3–4 cups sugar
1 tablespoon fresh lemon juice

In a medium pot, combine oranges and water. Bring to a boil and simmer for 30 minutes. Measure cooked oranges and combine with 1 part sugar to 1 part oranges (if your oranges measure 3 cups, combine with 3 cups sugar). Return oranges to the pot, stir in lemon juice, and simmer an additional 30 minutes. Cool to room temperature before using.

If after chilling the marmalade becomes too thick to spread easily, thin with a few tablespoons of hot water.

The preserve keeps for one week in the refrigerator.

Lingonberry Preserve
LINGONSYLT

The Swedish lingonberries are similar to but different from American cranberries. Swedish lingonberries are much smaller and deep red inside, not white inside like cranberries, creating a different preserve. Lingonberries are available fresh in North America only in the regions where they grow wild—Maine and Canada.

Lingonberry preserve is eaten with many savory dishes (meatballs, page 49) and sweet dishes (Swedish pancakes, page 118).

1 package (12 ounces–3 cups) cranberries, rinsed and picked over
1 cup water
1 cup sugar

In a medium saucepan combine cranberries and water. Boil over medium heat for 10–15 minutes. Remove from heat and add sugar; stir until sugar is dissolved. Let cool. Transfer to refrigerator. Serve as is.

Cranberry Relish

RÅRÖRD LINGONSYLT

Because the widely available cranberries in the United States are different from true lingonberries, I prefer them in an uncooked relish. This side dish is wonderful with savory dishes such as roast chicken (page 56) or roasted rack of lamb (page 44).

1 package (12 ounces–3 cups) cranberries, rinsed and picked over
1 whole orange, peel on, cut into large chunks
1 lemon, peel on, cut into large chunks
½ cup sugar

In a food processor, blend all ingredients until well mixed. Transfer to refrigerator and let sit for a minimum of 1 hour before serving.

Absolut Cranberries with Lavender Honey
LINGONSYLT MED VODKA

1 cup cranberries (4 ounces)
2 tablespoons vodka, preferably Absolut
3 tablespoons lavender honey (or 3 tablespoons honey and 1 sprig organic lavender flower)
1 tablespoon sugar

Combine all ingredients in a small saucepan and cook over medium heat for about 10 minutes or until cranberries begin to burst. Transfer to a bowl and chill until ready to serve.

NOTES

Index

Helene Henderson was born and raised in northern Sweden, where her love of cooking began. Now living in Los Angeles, she has worked in the movie industry and as a personal chef. She runs the catering business Lavender Farms and is a master gardener.